Genetic Algorithms
in Java Basics

Lee Jacobson
Burak Kanber

Apress®

ISBN-13 (pbk): 978-1-4842-0329-3

ISBN-13 (electronic): 978-1-4842-0328-6

Managing Director: Welmoed Spahr
Lead Editor: Steve Anglin
Technical Reviewer: John Zukowski and Massimo Nardone
Editorial Board: Steve Anglin, Louise Corrigan, Jim DeWolf, Jonathan Gennick, Robert Hutchinson, Michelle Lowman, James Markham, Susan McDermott, Matthew Moodie, Jeffrey Pepper, Douglas Pundick, Ben Renow-Clarke, Gwenan Spearing
Coordinating Editor: Jill Balzano
Compositor: SPi Global
Indexer: SPi Global
Artist: SPi Global

Distributed to the book trade worldwide by Springer Science + Business Media New York, 233 Spring Street, 6th Floor, New York, NY 10013. Phone 1-800-SPRINGER, fax (201) 348-4505, e-mail orders-ny@springer-sbm.com, or visit www.springer.com. Apress Media, LLC is a California LLC and the sole member (owner) is Springer Science + Business Media Finance Inc (SSBM Finance Inc). SSBM Finance Inc is a **Delaware** corporation.

For information on translations, please e-mail rights@apress.com, or visit www.apress.com.

Apress and friends of ED books may be purchased in bulk for academic, corporate, or promotional use. eBook versions and licenses are also available for most titles. For more information, reference our Special Bulk Sales–eBook Licensing web page at www.apress.com/bulk-sales.

Any source code or other supplementary material referenced by the author in this text is available to readers at www.apress.com. For detailed information about how to locate your book's source code, go to www.apress.com/source-code/.

Contents at a Glance

Contents

Contents

About the Authors

Lee Jacobson is a professional freelance software developer from Bristol, England who first began writing code at the age of 15 while trying to write his own games. His interest soon transitioned to software development and computer science which led him to the field of artificial intelligence. He found a passion for the subject after studying Genetic Algorithms and other optimization techniques at university. He would often enjoy spending his evenings learning about optimization algorithms such as genetic algorithms and how he could use them to solve various problems.

Burak Kanber is a New York City native and attended The Cooper Union for the Advancement of Science and Art. He earned both a Bachelor's and a Master's degree in Mechanical Engineering, concentrating on control systems, robotics, automotive engineering, and hybrid vehicle systems engineering. Software, however, had been a lifelong passion and consistent thread throughout Burak's life.

Burak began consulting with startups in New York City while attending The Cooper Union, helping companies develop core technology on a variety of platforms and in various industries. Exposure to art and design at The Cooper Union also helped Burak develop an eye and taste for product design.

Since founding Tidal Labs in 2009—a technology company that makes award-winning software for enterprise influencer management and content marketing–Burak has honed his skills in DevOps, Product Development, and Machine Learning.

Burak enjoys evenings at home in New York with his wonderful fiancée and their cat Luna.

About the Technical Reviewers

Massimo Nardone holds a Master of Science degree in Computing Science from the University of Salerno, Italy. He worked as a PCI QSA and Senior Lead IT Security/Cloud/SCADA Architect for many years, and currently works as the Security, Cloud and SCADA Lead IT Architect for Hewlett Packard Finland. He has more than 20 years of work experience in IT, including Security, SCADA, Cloud Computing, IT Infrastructure, Mobile, Security and WWW technology areas for both national and international projects. Massimo has worked as a Project Manager, Cloud/SCADA Lead IT Architect, Software Engineer, Research Engineer, Chief Security Architect, and Software Specialist. He worked as visiting lecturer and supervisor for exercises at the Networking Laboratory of the Helsinki University of Technology (Aalto University). He has been programming and teaching how to program with Perl, PHP, Java, VB, Python, C/C++ and MySQL for more than 20 years. He is the author of Beginning PHP and MySQL (Apress, 2014) and Pro Android Games (Apress, 2015).

He holds four international patents (PKI, SIP, SAML and Proxy areas).

John Zukowski is currently a software engineer with TripAdivsor, the world's largest travel site (www.tripadvisor.com). He has been playing with Java technologies for twenty years now and is the author of ten Java-related books. His books cover Java 6, Java Swing, Java Collections, and JBuilder from Apress, Java AWT from O'Reilly, and introductory Java from Sybex. He lives outside Boston, Massachusetts and has a Master's degree in software engineering from The Johns Hopkins University. You can follow him on Twitter at http://twitter.com/javajohnz.

Preface

The field of machine learning has grown immensely in popularity in recent years. There are, of course, many reasons for this, but the steady advancement of processing power, steadily falling costs of RAM and storage space, and the rise of on-demand cloud computing are certainly significant contributors.

But those factors only enabled the rise of machine learning; they don't explain it. What is it about machine learning that's so compelling? Machine learning is like an iceberg; the tip is made of novel and exciting areas of research like computer vision, speech recognition, bioinformatics, medical research, and even computers that can win a game of Jeopardy! (IBM's Watson). These fields are not to be downplayed or understated; they will absolutely become huge market drivers in years to come.

However, there is a large underwater portion of the iceberg that is mature enough to be useful to us today—though it's rare to see young engineers claiming "business intelligence" as their motivation for studying the field. Machine learning—yes, machine learning as it stands today—lets businesses learn from complex customer behavior. Machine learning helps us understand the stock market, weather patterns, crowd behavior at crowded concert venues, and can even be used to predict where the next flu breakout will be.

In fact, as processing resources become ever cheaper, it's hard to imagine a future where machine learning doesn't play a central role in most businesses' customer pipeline, operations, production, and growth strategies.

There is, however, a problem. Machine learning is a complex and difficult field with a high dropout rate. It takes time and effort to develop expertise. We're faced with a difficult but important task: we need to make machine learning more accessible in order to keep up with growing demand for experts in the field. So far, we're behind the curve. McKinsey & Company's 2011 "Big Data Whitepaper" estimated that demand for talent in machine learning will be 50-60% greater than its supply by the year 2018! While this puts existing machine learning experts in a great position for the next several years, it also hinders our ability to realize the full effects of machine learning in the near future.

Why Genetic Algorithms?

Genetic algorithms are a subset of machine learning. In practice, a genetic algorithm is typically not the single best algorithm you can use to solve a single, specific problem. There's almost always a better, more targeted solution to any individual problem! So why bother? Genetic algorithms are an excellent multi-tool that can be applied to many different types of problems. It's the difference between a Swiss Army knife and a proper ratcheting screwdriver. If your job is to tighten 300 screws, you'll want to spring for the screwdriver, but if your job is to tighten a few screws, cut some cloth, punch a hole in a piece of leather, and then open a cold bottle of soda to reward yourself for your hard work, the Swiss Army knife is the better bet.

Additionally, I believe that genetic algorithms are the best introduction to the study of machine learning as whole. If machine learning is an iceberg, genetic algorithms are part of the tip. Genetic algorithms are interesting, exciting, and novel. Genetic algorithms, being modeled on natural biological processes, make a connection between the computing world and the natural world. Writing your first genetic algorithm and watching astounding results appear from the chaos and randomness is awe-inspiring for many students.

Other fields of study at the tip of the machine learning iceberg are equally as exciting, but they tend to be more narrowly focused and more difficult to comprehend. Genetic algorithms, on the other hand, are easy to understand, are fun to implement, and they introduce many concepts used by all machine learning techniques.

If you are interested in machine learning but have no idea where to start, start with genetic algorithms. You'll learn important concepts that you'll carry over to other fields, you'll build—no, you'll earn—a great multi-tool that you can use to solve many types of problems, and you won't have to study advanced math to comprehend it.

About the Book

This book gives you an easy, straightforward introduction to genetic algorithms. There are no prerequisites in terms of math, data structures, or algorithms required to get the most out of this book—though we do expect that you are comfortable with computer programming at the intermediate level. While the programming language used here is Java, we don't use any Java-specific advanced language constructs or third party libraries. As long as you're comfortable with object-oriented programming, you'll have no problem following the examples here. By the end of this book, you'll be able to comfortably implement genetic algorithms in your language of choice, whether it's an object-oriented language, a functional one, or a procedural one.

This book will walk you through solving four different problems using genetic algorithms. Along the way, you'll pick up a number of techniques that you can mix and match when building genetic algorithms in the future. Genetic algorithms, of course, is a large and mature field that also has an underlying mathematical formality, and it's impossible to cover everything about the field in a single book. So we draw a line: we leave pedantry out of the discussion, we avoid mathematical formality, and we don't enter the realm of advanced genetic algorithms. This book is all about getting you up and running quickly with practical examples, and giving you enough of a foundation to continue study of advanced topics on your own.

The Source Code

The code presented in this book is comprehensive; everything you need to get the examples to run is printed in these pages. However, to save space and paper, we often omit code comments and Java docblocks when showing examples. Please visit http://www.apress.com/9781484203293 and open the Source Code/Downloads tab to download the accompanying Eclipse project that contains all of the example code in this book—you'll find a lot of helpful comments and docblocks that you won't find printed in these pages.

By reading this book and working its examples, you're taking your first step toward ultimately becoming an expert in machine learning. It may change the course of your career, but that's up to you. We can only do our best to educate and give you the tools that you need to build your own future. Good luck!

—Burak Kanber

Introduction   Chapter 1

Digital computers and the rise of the information age have revolutionized the modern lifestyle. The invention of digital computers has enabled us to digitize numerous areas of our lives. This digitalization allows us to outsource many tedious daily tasks to computers where previously humans may have been required. An everyday example of this would be modern word processing applications that feature built in spell checkers to automatically check documents for spelling and grammar mistakes.

As computers have grown faster and more computationally powerful, we have been able to use them to perform increasingly complex tasks such as understanding human speech and even somewhat accurately predict the weather. This constant innovation allows us to outsource a growing number of tasks to computers. A present day computer is likely able to execute billions of operations a second, but however technically capable they become, unless they can learn and adapt themselves to better suit the problems presented to them, they'll always be limited to whatever rules or code us humans write for them.

The field of artificial intelligence and the subset of genetic algorithms are beginning to tackle some of these more complex problems faced in today's digital world. By implementing genetic algorithms into real world applications it is possible to solve problems which would be nearly impossible to solve by more traditional computing methods.

What is Artificial Intelligence?

In 1950, Alan Turing – a mathematician and early computer-scientist - wrote a famous paper titled, "Computing Machinery and Intelligence", where he questioned, "Can computers think?" His question caused much debate on what intelligence actually is and what the fundamental limitations of computers might be.

Many early computer scientists believed computers would not only be able to demonstrate intelligent-like behavior, but that they would achieve human level intelligence in just a few decades of research. This notion is indicated by Herbert A. Simon in 1965 when he declared, "Machines will be capable, within twenty years, of doing any work a man can do." Of course now, over 50 years later, we know that

Simon's prediction was far from reality, but at the time many computer scientists agreed with his position and made it their goal to create a "strong AI" machine. A strong AI machine is simply a machine which is at least just as intellectually capable at completing any task it's given as humans.

Today, more than 50 years since Alan Turing's famous question was posed, the possibility of whether machines will eventually be able to think in a similar way to humans still remains largely unanswered. To this day his paper, and thoughts, on what it means to "think" is still widely debated by philosophers and computer scientists alike.

Although we're still far from creating machines able to replicate the intelligence of humans, we have undoubtedly made significant advances in artificial intelligence over the last few decades. Since the 1950s the focus on "strong AI" and developing artificial intelligence comparable to that of humans, has begun shifting in favor of "weak AI". Weak AI is the development of more narrowly focused intelligent machines which is much more achievable in the short term. This narrower focus has allowed computer scientists to create practical and seemingly intelligent systems such as Apple's Siri and Google's self-driving car, for example.

When creating a weak AI system, researchers will typically focus on building a system or machine which is only just as "intelligent" as it needs to be to complete a relatively small problem. This means we can apply simpler algorithms and use less computing power while still achieving results. In comparison, strong AI research focuses on building a machine that's intelligent and able enough to tackle any problem which we humans can. This makes building a final product using strong AI much less practical due to the scope of the problem.

In only a few decades' weak AI systems have become a common component of our modern lifestyle. From playing chess, to helping humans fly fighter jets, weak AI systems have proven themselves useful in solving problems once thought only possible by humans. As digital computers become smaller and more computationally capable, the usefulness of these systems is likely to only increase in time.

Biologically Analogies

When early computer scientists were first trying to build artificially intelligent systems, they would frequently look to nature for inspiration on how their algorithms could work. By creating models which mimic processes found in nature, computer scientists were able to give their algorithms the ability to evolve, and even replicate characteristics of the human brain. It was implementing their biologically-inspired algorithms that enabled these early pioneers, for the first time, to give their machines the ability to adapt, learn and control aspects of their environments.

By using different biological analogies as a guiding metaphor to develop artificially intelligent systems, computer scientists created distinct fields of research. Naturally, the different biological systems that inspired each field of research have their own specific advantages and applications. One successful field, and the one we're paying attention to in this book, is evolutionary computation - in which genetic algorithms make up the majority of the research. Other fields focused on slightly different areas, such as modeling the human brain. This field of research is called artificial neural networks, and it uses models of the biological nervous system to mimic its learning and data processing capabilities.

History of Evolutionary Computation

Evolutionary computation was first explored as an optimization tool in the 1950s when computer scientists were playing with the idea of applying Darwinian ideas of biological evolution to a population of candidate solutions. They theorized that it may be possible to apply evolutionary operators such as crossover – which is an analog to biological reproduction - and mutation – which is the process in which new genetic information is added to the genome. It's these operators when coupled with selection pressure that provide genetic algorithms the ability to "evolve" new solutions when left over a period of time.

In the 1960s "evolution strategies" – an optimization technique applying the ideas of natural selection and evolution - was first proposed by Rechenberg (1965, 1973) and his ideas were later expanded on by Schwefel (1975, 1977). Other computer scientists at the time were working independently on similar fields of research such as Fogel L.J; Owens, A.J; and Walsh, M.J (1966), who were the first to introduce the field of evolutionary programming. Their technique involved representing candidate solutions as finite-state machines and applying mutation to create new solutions.

During the 1950s and 1960s some biologists studying evolution began experimenting with simulating evolution using computers. However, it was Holland, J.H. (1975) who first invented and developed the concept of genetic algorithms during the 1960s and 1970s. He finally presented his ideas in 1975 in his groundbreaking book, "Adaption in Natural and Artificial Systems". Holland's book demonstrated how Darwinian evolution could be abstracted and modeled using computers for use in optimization strategies. His book explained how biological chromosomes can be modeled as strings of 1s and 0s, and how populations of these chromosomes can be "evolved" by implementing techniques that are found in natural selection such as mutation, selection and crossover.

Holland's original definition of a genetic algorithm has gradually changed over the decades from when it was first introduced back in the 1970s. This is somewhat due to recent researchers working in the field of evolutionary computation occasionally bringing ideas from the different approaches together. Although this has blurred the lines between many of the methodologies it has provided us with rich set of tools which can help us better tackle specific problems. The term "genetic algorithm" in this book will be used to refer to both Holland's classical vision of a genetic algorithm, and also to the wider, present day, interpretation of the words.

Computer scientists to this day are still looking at biology and biological systems to give them ideas on how they can create better algorithms. One of the more recent biologically inspired optimization algorithms would be Ant Colony Optimization which was first proposed in 1992 by Marco, D. (1992). Ant Colony optimization models the behavior of ants as a method for solving various optimization problems such as the Traveling Salesman Problem.

The Advantage of Evolutionary Computation

The very rate at which intelligent machines have been adopted within our society is an acknowledgement of their usefulness. The vast majority of problems we use computers to solve can be reduced to relatively simple static decision problems. These problems can become rapidly more complex as the amount of possible inputs and outputs increase, and only further complicated when the solution needs to adapt to a changing problem. In addition to this, some problems may also require an algorithm to search through a huge number of possible solutions in an attempt to find a feasible solution. Depending on the amount of solutions that need to be searched through, classical computational methods may not be able find a feasible solution in the timeframe available – even using a super computer. It's in these circumstances where evolutionary computation can offer a helping hand.

To give you an idea of a typical problem we can solve with classical computational methods, consider a traffic light system. Traffic lights are relatively simple systems which only require a basic level of intelligence to operate. A traffic light system will usually have just a few inputs which can alert it to events such as a car or pedestrian waiting to use the junction. It then needs to manage those inputs and correctly change the lights in a way in which cars and pedestrians can use the junction efficiently without causing any accidents. Although, there may be a certain amount of knowledge required to operate a traffic light system, its inputs and outputs are basic enough that a set of instructions to operate the traffic light system can be designed and programmed by humans without much problem.

Often we will need an intelligent system to handle more complex inputs and outputs. This could mean it is no longer as simple, or maybe impossible, for a human to program a set of instructions so the machine can correctly map the inputs to a viable output. In these cases where the complexity of the problem makes it unpractical for a human programmer to solve with code, optimization and learning algorithms can provide us with a method to use the computer's processing power to find a solution to the problem itself. An example of this might be when building a fraud detection system that can recognize fraudulent transactions based on transaction information. Although a relationship may occur between the transaction data and a fraudulent transaction, it could depend on many subtleties within the data itself. It's these subtle patterns in the input that might be hard for a human to code for, making it a good candidate for applying evolutionary computation.

Evolutionary algorithms are also useful when humans don't know how to solve a problem. A classic example of this was when NASA was looking for an antenna design that met all their requirements for a 2006 space mission. NASA wrote a genetic algorithm which evolved an antenna design to meet all of their specific design constraints such as, signal quality, size, weight and cost. In this example NASA didn't know how to design an antenna which would fit all their requirements, so they decided to write a program which could evolve one instead.

Another situation in which we may want to apply an evolutionary computation strategy is when the problem is constantly changing, requiring an adaptive solution. This problem can be found when building an algorithm to make predictions on the stock market. An algorithm that makes accurate predictions about the stock market one week might not make accurate predictions the following week. This is due to the forever shifting patterns and trends of the stock market and thus making prediction algorithms very unreliable unless they're able to quickly adapt to the changing patterns as they occur. Evolutionary computation can help accommodate for these changes by providing a method in which adaptations can be made to the prediction algorithm as necessary.

Finally, some problems require searching through a large, or possibly, infinite amount of potential solutions to find the best, or good enough, solution for the problem faced. Fundamentally, all evolutionary algorithms can be viewed as search algorithms which search through a set of possible solutions looking the best – or "fittest" - solution. You may be able to visualize this if you think of all the potential combinations of genes found in an organism's genome as candidate solutions. Biological evolution is great at searching through these possible genetic sequences to find a solution which sufficiently suits its environment. In larger search spaces it's likely - even when using evolutionary algorithms - the best solution to a given problem won't be found. However, this is rarely an issue for most optimization problems because typically we only require a solution good enough to get the job done.

The approach provided by evolutionary computation can be thought of as a "bottom-up" paradigm. That is when all the complexity that emerges from an algorithm comes from simple, underlying, rules. The alternative to this would be a "top-down" approach which would require all the complexity demonstrated within the algorithm to be written by humans. Genetic algorithms are fairly simple to develop; making them an appealing choice when otherwise a complex algorithm is required to solve the problem.

Here is a list of features which can make a problem a good candidate for an evolutionary algorithm:

- If the problem is sufficiently hard to write code to solve

- When a human isn't sure how to solve the problem

- If a problem is constantly changing

- When it's not feasible to search through each possible solution

- When a "good-enough" solution is acceptable

Biological Evolution

Biological evolution, through the process of natural selection, was first proposed by Charles Darwin (1859) in his book, "The Origin of Species". It was his concept of biological evolution which inspired early computer scientists to adapt and use biological evolution as a model for their optimization techniques, found in evolutionary computation algorithms.

Because many of the ideas and concepts used in genetic algorithms stem directly from biological evolution, a basic familiarity with the subject is useful for a deeper understanding into the field. With that being said, before we begin exploring genetic algorithms, let's first run through the (somewhat simplified) basics of biological evolution.

All organisms contain DNA which encodes all of the different traits that make up that organism. DNA can be thought of as life's instruction manual to create the organism from scratch. Changing the DNA of an organism will change its traits such as eye and hair color. DNA is made up of individual genes, and it is these genes that are responsible for encoding the specific traits of an organism.

An organism's genes are grouped together in chromosomes and a complete set of chromosomes make up an organism's genome. All organisms will have a least one chromosome, but usually contain many more, for example humans have 46 chromosomes with some species, having more than 1000! In genetic algorithms we usually refer to the chromosome as the candidate solution. This is because genetic algorithms typically use a single chromosome to encode the candidate solution.

The various possible settings for a specific trait are called an "allele", and the position in the chromosome where that trait is encoded is called a "locus". We refer to a specific genome as a "genotype" and the physical organism that genotype encodes is called the "phenotype".

When two organisms mate, DNA from both organisms are brought together and combined in such a way that the resulting organism – usually referred to as the offspring – acquires 50% of its DNA from its first parent, and the other 50% from the second. Every so often a gene from the organisms DNA will mutate providing it with DNA found in neither of its parents. These mutations provide the population with genetic diversity by adding genes to the population that weren't available beforehand. All possible genetic information in the population is referred as the population's "gene pool".

If the resulting organism is fit enough to survive in its environment it's likely to mate itself, allowing its DNA to continue on into future populations. If however, the resulting organism isn't fit enough to survive and eventually mate its genetic material won't propagate into future populations. This is why evolution is occasionally referred to as survival of the fittest – only the fittest individuals survive and pass on their DNA. It's this selective pressure that slowly guides evolution to find increasingly fitter and better adapted individuals.

An Example of Biological Evolution

To help clarify how this process will gradually lead to the evolution of increasingly fitter individuals, consider the following example:

On a distant planet there exists a species that takes the shape of a white square.

The white square species has lived for thousands of years in peace, until recently when a new species arrived, the black circle.

The black circle species were carnivores and began feeding on the white square population.

The white squares didn't have any way to defend themselves against the black circles. Until one day, one of the surviving white squares randomly mutated from a white square into a black square. The black circle no longer saw the new black square as food because it was the same color as itself.

Some of the surviving square population mated, creating a new generation of squares. Some of these new squares inherited the black square color gene.

However, the white colored squares continued to be eaten…

Eventually, thanks to their evolutionary advantage of looking similar to the black circle, they were no longer eaten. Now the only color of square left was the black square.

No longer prey to the black circle, the black squares were once again free to live in peace.

Basic Terminology

Genetic algorithms were built on the concepts of biological evolution, so if you're familiar with the terminology found in evolution, you'll likely notice overlap in the terminology found when working with genetic algorithms. The similarities between the fields are of course due to evolutionary algorithms, and more specifically, genetic algorithms being analogous to processes found in nature.

Terms

It's important that before we go deeper into the field of genetic algorithms we first understand some of the basic language and terminology used. As the book progresses, more complex terminology will be introduced as required. Below is a list of some of the more common terms for reference.

- Population - This is simply just a collection of candidate solutions which can have genetic operators such as mutation and crossover applied to them.

- Candidate Solution – A possible solution to a given problem.

- Gene – The indivisible building blocks making up the chromosome. Classically a gene consists of 0 or a 1.

- Chromosome – A chromosome is a string of genes. A chromosome defines a specific candidate solution. A typical chromosome with a binary encoding might contain something like, "01101011".

- Mutation – The process in which genes in a candidate solution are randomly altered to create new traits.

- Crossover – The process in which chromosomes are combined to create a new candidate solution. This is sometimes referred to as recombination.

- Selection – This is the technique of picking candidate solutions to breed the next generation of solutions.

- Fitness – A score which measures the extent to which a candidate solution is adapted to suit a given problem.

Search Spaces

In computer science when dealing with optimization problems that have many candidate solutions which need to be searched through, we refer to the collection of solutions as a "search space". Each specific point within the search space serves as a candidate solution for the given problem. Within this search space there is a concept of distance where solutions that are placed closer to one another are more likely to express similar traits than solutions place further apart. To understand how these distances are organized on the search space, consider the following example using a binary genetic representation:

"101" is only 1 difference away from, "111". This is because there is only 1 change required (flipping the 0 to 1) to transition from "101" to "111". This means these solutions are only 1 space apart on the search space.

"000" on the other hand, is three differences away from, "111". This gives it a distance of 3, placing "000" 3 spaces from "111" on the search space.

Because solutions with fewer changes are grouped nearer to one another, the distance between solutions on the search space can be used to provide an approximation of the characteristics held by another solution. This understanding is often used as a tactic by many search algorithms to improve their search results.

Fitness Landscapes

When candidate solutions found within the search space are labeled by their individual fitness levels we can begin to think of the search space as a "fitness landscape". Figure 1-1 provides an example of what a 2D fitness landscape might look like.

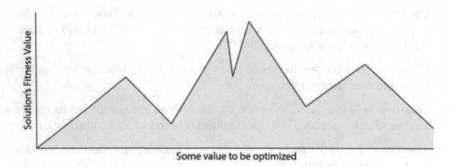

Figure 1-1. A 2D fitness landscape

On the bottom axis of our fitness landscape is the value we're optimizing for, and on the left axis is its corresponding fitness value. I should note, this is typically an over simplification of what would be found in practice. Most real world applications have multiple values that need optimizing creating a multi-dimensional fitness landscape.

In the above example the fitness value for every candidate solution in the search space can be seen. This makes it easy to see where the fittest solution is located, however, for this to be possible in reality, each candidate solution in the search space would have needed to have their fitness function evaluated. For complex problems with exponential search spaces it just isn't plausible to evaluate every solution's fitness value. In these cases, it is the search algorithm's job to find where the best solution likely resides while being limited to only having a tiny proportion of the search space visible. Figure 1-2 is an example of what a search algorithm might typically see.

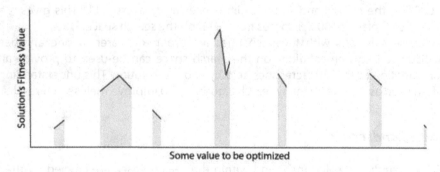

Figure 1-2. A more typical search fitness space

Consider an algorithm that is searching through a search space of one billion (1,000,000,000) possible solutions. Even if each solution only takes 1 second to evaluate and be assigned a fitness value, it would still take over 30 years to explicitly search through each potential solution! If we don't know the fitness value for each solution in the search space then we are unable to definitively know where the best solution resides. In this case, the only reasonable approach is to use a search algorithm capable of finding a good-enough, solution in the time frame available. In these conditions, genetic algorithms and evolutionary algorithms in general, are very effective at finding feasible, near optimum solutions in a relatively short time frame.

Genetic algorithms use a population approach when searching the search space. As part of their search strategy genetic algorithms will assume two well ranking solutions can be combined to form an even fitter offspring. This process can be visualized on our fitness landscape (Figure 1-3).

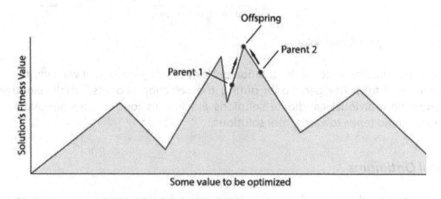

Figure 1-3. Parent and offspring in the fitness plot

The mutation operator found in genetic algorithms allows us to search the close neighbors of the specific candidate solution. When mutation is applied to a gene its value is randomly changed. This can be pictured by taking a single step on the search space (Figure 1-4).

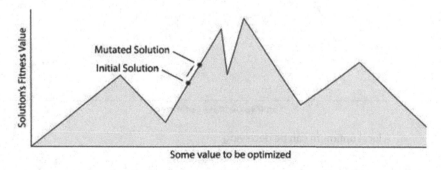

Figure 1-4. A fitness plot showing the mutation

In the example of both crossover and mutation it is possible to end up with a solution less fit than what we originally set out with (Figure 1-5).

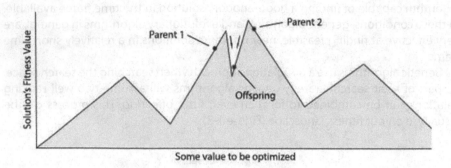

Figure 1-5. A poor fitness solution

In these circumstances, if the solution performs poorly enough, it will eventually be removed from the gene pool during the selection process. Small negative changes in individual candidate solutions are fine as long as the population's average trend tends towards fitter solutions.

Local Optimums

An obstacle that should be considered when implementing an optimization algorithm is how well the algorithm can escape from locally optimal positions in the search space. To better visualize what a local optimum is, refer to Figure 1-6.

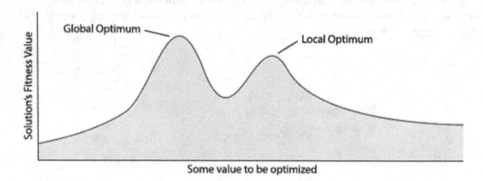

Figure 1-6. A local optimum can be deceiving

Here we can see two hills on the fitness landscape which have peaks of slightly different heights. As mentioned earlier, the optimization algorithm isn't able to see the entire fitness landscape, and instead, the best it can do is find solutions which it believes are likely to be in an optimal position on the search space. It's because of this characteristic the optimization algorithm can often unknowingly focus its search on suboptimal portions of the search space.

This problem becomes quickly noticeable when implementing a simple hill climbing algorithm to solve problems of any sufficient complexity. A simple hill climber doesn't have any inherent method to deal with local optimums, and as a result will often terminate its search in locally optimal regions of the search space. A simple stochastic hill climber is comparable to a genetic algorithm without a population and crossover. The algorithm is fairly easy to understand, it starts off at a random point in the search space, then attempts to find a better solution by evaluating its neighbor solutions. When the hill climber finds a better solution amongst its neighbors, it will move to the new position and restart the search process again. This process will gradually find improved solutions by taking steps up whatever hill it found itself on in the search space – hence the name, hill climber. When the hill climber can no longer find a better solution it will assume it is at the top of the hill and stop the search.

Figure 1-7 illustrates how a typical run-through of a hill climber algorithm might look.

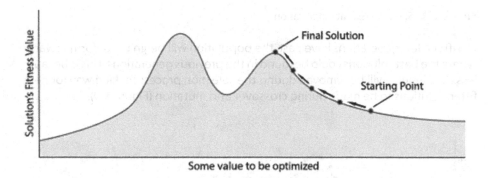

Figure 1-7. Shows how the hill climber works

The diagram above demonstrates how a simple hill climber algorithm can easily return a locally optimal solution if it's search begins in a locally optimal area of the search space.

Although there isn't any guaranteed way to avoid local optimums without first evaluating the entire search area, there are many variations of the algorithm which can help avoid local optimums. One of the most basic and effective methods is called random-restart hill climbing, which simply runs the hill climbing algorithm multiple times from random starting positions then returns the best solution found from its various runs. This optimization method is relatively easy to implement and surprisingly effective. Other approaches such as, Simulated Annealing (see Kirkpatrick, Gelatt, and Vecchi (1983)) and Tabu search (see Glover (1989) and Glover (1990)) are slight variations to the hill climbing algorithm which both having properties that can help reduce local optimums.

Genetic algorithms are surprisingly effective at avoiding local optimums and retrieving solutions that are close to optimal. One of the ways it achieves this is by having a population that allows it to sample a large area of the search space locating the best areas to continue the search. Figure 1-8 shows how the population might be distributed at initialization.

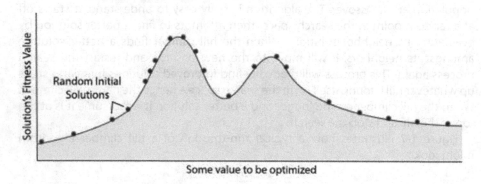

Figure 1-8. Sample areas at initialization

After a few generations have past, the population will begin to conform towards where the best solutions could be found in the previous generations. This is because less fit solutions will be removed during the selection process making way for new, fitter, solutions to be made during crossover and mutation (Figure 1-9).

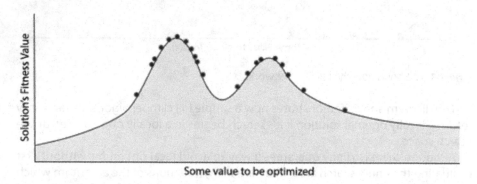

Figure 1-9. The fitness diagram after some generations have mutated

The mutation operator also plays a role in evading local optimums. Mutation allows a solution to jump from its current position to another position on the search space. This process will often lead to the discovery of fitter solutions in more optimal areas in the search space.

Parameters

Although all genetic algorithms are based on the same concepts, their specific implementations can vary quite a bit. One of the ways specific implementations can vary is by their parameters. A basic genetic algorithm will have at least a few parameters that need to be considered during the implementation. The main three are the rate of mutation, the population size and the third is the crossover rate.

Mutation Rate

The mutation rate is the probability in which a specific gene in a solution's chromosome will be mutated. There is technically no correct value for the mutation rate of a genetic algorithm, but some mutation rates will provide vastly better results than others. A higher mutation rate allows for more genetic diversity in the population and can also help the algorithm avoid local optimums. However, a mutation rate that's too high can cause too much genetic variation between each generation causing it to lose good solutions it found in its previous population.

If the mutation rate is too low, the algorithm can take an unreasonably long time to move along the search space hindering its ability to find a satisfactory solution. A mutation rate that's too high can also prolong the time it takes to find an acceptable solution. Although, a high mutation rate can help the genetic algorithm avoid getting stuck in local optimums, when it's set too high it can have a negative impact on the search. This, as was said before, is due to the solutions in each generation being mutated to such a large extent that they're practically randomized after mutation has been applied.

To understand why a well configured mutation rate is important, consider two binary encoded candidate solutions, "100" and "101". Without mutation new solutions can only come from crossover. However, when we crossover our solutions there are only two possible outcomes available for the offspring, "100" or "101". This is because the only difference in the parent's genome's can be found in their last bits. If the offspring receives its last bit from the first parent, it will be a "1", otherwise if it's from the second, it would be a "0". If the algorithm needed to find an alternative solution it would need to mutate an existing solution, giving it new genetic information that isn't available elsewhere in the gene pool.

The mutation rate should be set to a value that allows for enough diversity to prevent the algorithm plateauing, but not so much that it causes the algorithm to lose valuable genetic information from the previous population. This balance will depend on the nature of the problem being solved.

Population Size

The population size is simply the number of individuals in the genetic algorithm's population in any one generation. The larger the population's size, the more of the search space the algorithm can sample. This will help lead it in the direction of more accurate, and globally optimal, solutions. A small population size will often result in the algorithm finding less desirable solutions in locally optimal areas of the search space, however they require less computational resources per generation.

Again here, like with the mutation rate, a balance needs to be found for optimum performance of the genetic algorithm. Likewise, the population size required will change depending on the nature of the problem being solved. Large hilly search spaces commonly require a larger population size to find the best solutions. Interestingly, when picking a population size there is a point in which increasing the size will cease to provide the algorithm with much improvement in the accuracy of the solutions it finds. Instead, it will slow the execution down due to the extra computational demand needed to process the additional individuals. A population size around this transition is usually going to provide the best balance between resources and results.

Crossover Rate

The frequency in which crossover is applied also has an effect on the overall performance of the genetic algorithm. Changing the crossover rate adjusts the chance in which solutions in the population will have the crossover operator applied to them. A high rate allows for many new, potentially superior, solutions to be found during the crossover phase. A lower rate will help keep the genetic information from fitter individuals intact for the next generation. The crossover rate should usually be set to a reasonably high rate promoting the search for new solutions while allowing a small percentage of the population to be kept unaffected for the next generation.

Genetic Representations

Aside from the parameters, another component that can affect a genetic algorithm's performance is the genetic representation used. This is the way the genetic information is encoded within the chromosomes. Better representations will encode the solution in a way that is expressive while also being easily evolvable. Holland's (1975) genetic algorithm was based on a binary genetic representation. He proposed using chromosomes that were comprised of strings containing 0s and 1s. This binary representation is probably the simplest encoding available, however for many problems it isn't quite expressive enough to be a suitable first choice.

Consider the example in which a binary representation is used to encode an integer which is being optimized for use in some function. In this example, "000" represents 0, and "111" represents 7, as it typically would in binary. If the first gene in the chromosome is mutated - by flipping the bit from 0 to 1, or from 1 to 0 - it would change the encoded value by 4 ("111" = 7, "011" = 3). However, if the final gene in the chromosome is changed it will only effect the encoded value by 1 ("111" = 7, "110" = 6). Here the mutation operator has a different effect on the candidate solution depending on which gene in its chromosome is being operated on. This disparity isn't ideal as it will reduce performance and predictability of the algorithm. For this example, it would have been better to use an integer with a complimentary mutation operator which could add or subtract a relatively small amount to the gene's value.

Aside from simple binary representations and integers, genetic algorithms can use: floating point numbers, trees-based representations, objects, and any other data structure required for its genetic encoding. Picking the right representation is key when it comes to building an effective genetic algorithm.

Termination

Genetic algorithms can continue to evolve new candidate solutions for however long is necessary. Depending on the nature of the problem, a genetic algorithm could run for anywhere between a few seconds to many years! We call the condition in which a genetic algorithm finishes its search its termination condition.

Some typical termination conditions would be:

- A maximum number of generations is reached

- Its allocated time limit has been exceeded

- A solution has been found that meets the required criteria

- The algorithm has reached a plateau

Occasionally it might be preferable to implement multiple termination conditions. For example, it can be convenient to set a maximum time limit with the possibility of terminating earlier if an adequate solution is found.

The Search Process

To finish the chapter let's take a step-by-step look at the basic process behind a genetic algorithm, illustrated in Figure 1-10.

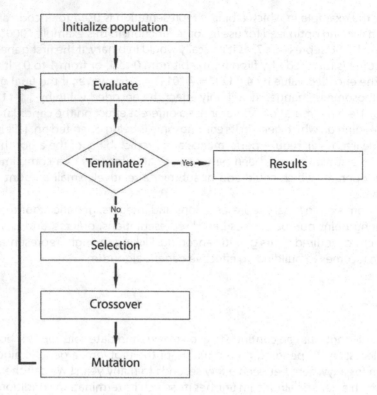

Figure 1-10. A general genetic algorithm process

1. Genetic algorithms begin by initializing a population of candidate solutions. This is typically done randomly to provide an even coverage of the entire search space.

2. Next, the population is evaluated by assigning a fitness value to each individual in the population. In this stage we would often want to take note of the current fittest solution, and the average fitness of the population.

3. After evaluation, the algorithm decides whether it should terminate the search depending on the termination conditions set. Usually this will be because the algorithm has reached a fixed number of generations or an adequate solution has been found.

4. If the termination condition is not met, the population goes through a selection stage in which individuals from the population are selected based on their fitness score – the higher the fitness, the better chance an individual has of being selected.

5. The next stage is to apply crossover and mutation to the selected individuals. This stage is where new individuals are created for the next generation.

6. At this point the new population goes back to the evaluation step and the process starts again. We call each cycle of this loop a generation.

7. When the termination condition is finally met, the algorithm will break out of the loop and typically return its finial search results back to the user.

CITATIONS

Turing, A.M. (1950). "Computing Machinery and Intelligence"

Simon, H.A. (1965). "The Shape of Automation for Men and Management"

Barricell, N.A. (1975). "Symbiogenetic Evolution Processes Realised by Artificial Methods"

Darwin, C. (1859). "On the Origin of Species"

Dorigo, M. (1992). "Optimization, Learning and Natural Algorithms"

Rechenberg, I. (1965) "Cybernetic Solution Path of an Experimental Problem"

Rechenberg, I. (1973) "Evolutionsstrategie: Optimierung technischer Systeme nach Prinzipien der biologischen Evolution"

Schwefel, H.-P. (1975) "Evolutionsstrategie und numerische Optimierung"

Schwefel, H.-P. (1977) "Numerische Optimierung von Computer-Modellen mittels der Evolutionsstrategie"

Fogel L.J; Owens, A.J; and Walsh, M.J. (1966) "Artificial Intelligence through Simulated Evolution"

Holland, J.H. (1975) "Adaptation in Natural and Artificial Systems"

Dorigo, M. (1992) "Optimization, Learning and Natural Algorithms"

Glover, F. (1989) "Tabu search. Part I"

Glover, F. (1990) "Tabu search. Part II"

Kirkpatrick, S; Gelatt, C.D, Jr., and Vecchi, M.P. (1983) "Optimization by simulated annealing"

Implementation of a Basic Genetic Algorithm

In this chapter we will begin to explore the techniques used to implement a basic genetic algorithm. The program we develop here will be modified adding features in the succeeding chapters in this book. We will also explore how the performance of a genetic algorithm can vary depending on its parameters and configuration.

To follow along with the code in this section you'll need to first have the Java JDK installed on your computer. You can download and install the Java JDK for free from the Oracle's website:

oracle.com/technetwork/java/javase/downloads/index.html

Although not necessary, in addition to installing the Java JDK, for convenience you may also choose to install a Java compatible IDE such as Eclipse or NetBeans.

Pre-Implementation

Before implementing a genetic algorithm it's a good idea to first consider if a genetic algorithm is the right approach for the task at hand. Often there will be better techniques to solve specific optimization problems, usually by taking advantage of some domain dependent heuristics. Genetic algorithms are domain independent, or "weak methods", which can be applied to problems without requiring any specific prior knowledge to assist with its search process. For this reason, if there isn't any known domain specific knowledge available to help guide the search process, a genetic algorithm can still be applied to discover potential solutions.

When it has been determined that a weak search method is appropriate, the type of weak method used should also be considered. This could simply be because an alternative method provides better results on average, but it could also be because an alternative method is easier to implement, requires less computational resources, or can find a good enough result in a shorter time period.

Pseudo Code for a Basic Genetic Algorithm

The pseudo code for a basic genetic algorithm is as follows:

```
1: generation = 0;
2: population[generation] = initializePopulation(populationSize);
3: evaluatePopulation(population[generation]);
3: While isTerminationConditionMet() == false do
4:     parents = selectParents(population[generation]);
5:    population[generation+1] = crossover(parents);
6:   population[generation+1] = mutate(population[generation+1]);
7:    evaluatePopulation(population[generation]);
8:     generation++;
9: End loop;
```

The pseudo code begins with creating the genetic algorithm's initial population. This population is then evaluated to find the fitness values of its individuals. Next, a check is run to decide if the genetic algorithm's termination condition has been met. If it hasn't, the genetic algorithm begins looping and the population goes through its first round of crossover and mutation before finally being reevaluated. From here, crossover and mutation are continuously applied until the termination condition is met, and the genetic algorithm terminates.

This pseudo code demonstrates the basic process of a genetic algorithm; however it is necessary that we look at each step in more detail to fully understand how to create a satisfactory genetic algorithm.

About the Code Examples in this Book

Each chapter in this book is represented as a package in the accompanying Eclipse project. Each package will have, at minimum, four classes:

- A GeneticAlgorithm class, which abstracts the genetic algorithm itself and provides problem-specific implementations of interface methods, such as crossover, mutation, fitness evaluation, and termination condition checking.

- An Individual class, which represents a single candidate solution and its chromosome.

- A Population class, which represents a population or a generation of Individuals, and applies group-level operations to them.

- A class that contains the "main" method, some bootstrap code, the concrete version of the pseudocode above, and any supporting work that a specific problem may need. These classes will be named according to the problem it solves, e.g. "AllOnesGA", "RobotController", etc.

The GeneticAlgorithm, Population, and Individual classes that you initially write in this chapter will need to be modified for each of the following chapters in this book.

You could imagine that these classes are actually concrete implementations of interfaces such as a GeneticAlgorithmInterface, PopulationInterface, and IndividualInterface–however, we've kept the layout of the Eclipse project simple and avoided using interfaces.

The GeneticAlgorithm classes you'll find throughout this book will always implement a number of important methods such as 'calcFitness', 'evalPopulation', 'isTerminationConditionMet', 'crossoverPopulation', and 'mutatePopulation'. However, the contents of these methods will be slightly different in each chapter, based on the requirements of the problem at hand.

While following the examples in this book we recommend copying the GeneticAlgorithm, Population, and Individual classes over to each new problem, as some methods' implementations will remain the same from chapter to chapter, but others will differ.

Also, be sure to read the comments in the source code in the attached Eclipse project! To save space in the book we've left long comments and docblocks out, but have taken great care to annotate the source code thoroughly in the Eclipse file available for download. It's like having a second book to read!

In many cases, the chapters in this book will ask you to add or modify a single method in a class. Generally, it doesn't matter where in a file you add a new method, so in these cases we'll either omit the rest of the class from the example, or we'll show function signatures only to help keep you on track.

Basic Implementation

To remove any unnecessary details and keep the initial implementation easy to follow, the first genetic algorithm we will cover in this book will be a simple binary genetic algorithm.

Binary genetic algorithms are relatively easy to implement and can be incredibly effective tools for solving a wide spectrum of optimization problems. As you may remember from Chapter 1, binary genetic algorithms were the original category of genetic algorithm proposed by Holland (1975).

The Problem

First, let's review the "all ones" problem, a very basic problem that can be solved using a binary genetic algorithm.

The problem isn't very interesting, but it serves its role as being a simple problem which helps emphasize the fundamental techniques involved. As the name suggests, the problem is simply finding a string which is comprised entirely of ones. So for a string with a length of 5 the best solution would be, "11111".

Parameters

Now we have a problem to solve, let's move on to the implementation. The first thing we're going to do is set up the genetic algorithm parameters. As covered previously, the three primary parameters are population size, mutation rate and crossover rate. We also introduce a concept called "elitism" in this chapter, and will include that as one of the parameters of the genetic algorithm.

To begin, create a class called GeneticAlgorithm. If you're using Eclipse, you can do this by selecting File ➤ New ➤ Class. We have chosen to name packages corresponding to the chapter number in this book, therefore we'll work in the package "Chapter2".

This GeneticAlgorithm class will contain the methods and variables needed for operations of the genetic algorithm itself. For example, this class includes the logic to handle crossover, mutation, fitness evaluation, and termination condition checking. After the class has been created, add a constructor which accepts the four parameters: population size, mutation rate, crossover rate, and number of elite members.

```java
package chapter2;
/**
 * Lots of comments in the source that are omitted here!
 */
public class GeneticAlgorithm {
      private int populationSize;
      private double mutationRate;
      private double crossoverRate;
      private int elitismCount;

public GeneticAlgorithm(int populationSize, double mutationRate, double
crossoverRate, int elitismCount) {
            this.populationSize = populationSize;
            this.mutationRate = mutationRate;
            this.crossoverRate = crossoverRate;
            this.elitismCount = elitismCount;
      }

      /**
       * Many more methods implemented later...
       */
}
```

When passed the required parameters, this constructor will create a new instance of the GeneticAlgorithm class with the required configuration.

Now we should create our bootstrap class – recall that each chapter will require a bootstrap class to initialize the genetic algorithm and provide a starting point for the application. Name this class "AllOnesGA" and define a "main" method:

```
package chapter2;
public class AllOnesGA {
    public static void main(String[] args) {
        // Create GA object
        GeneticAlgorithm ga = new GeneticAlgorithm(100, 0.01, 0.95, 0);
        // We'll add a lot more here...
    }
}
```

For the time being, we'll just use some typical values for the parameters, population size = 100; mutation rate = 0.01; crossover rate = 0.95, and an elitism count of 0 (effectively disabling it – for now). After you have completed your implementation at the end of the chapter, you can experiment with how changing these parameters affect the performance of the algorithm.

Initialization

Our next step is to initialize a population of potential solutions. This is usually done randomly, but occasionally it might be preferable to initialize the population more systematically, possibly to make use of known information about the search space. In this example, each individual in the population will be initialized randomly. We can do this by selecting a value of 1 or 0 for each gene in a chromosome at random.

Before initializing the population we need to create two classes, one to manage and create the population and the other to manage and create the population's individuals. It will be these classes that contain the methods to fetch an individual's fitness, or get the fittest individual in the population, for example.

First let's start by creating the Individual class. Note that we've omitted all the comments and method docblocks below to save paper! You can find a thoroughly annotated version of this class in the accompanying Eclipse project.

```
package chapter2;

public class Individual {
    private int[] chromosome;
    private double fitness = -1;

    public Individual(int[] chromosome) {
        // Create individual chromosome
        this.chromosome = chromosome;
    }
```

```java
    public Individual(int chromosomeLength) {
        this.chromosome = new int[chromosomeLength];
        for (int gene = 0; gene < chromosomeLength; gene++) {
            if (0.5 < Math.random()) {
                this.setGene(gene, 1);
            } else {
                this.setGene(gene, 0);
            }
        }

    }

    public int[] getChromosome() {
        return this.chromosome;
    }

    public int getChromosomeLength() {
        return this.chromosome.length;
    }

    public void setGene(int offset, int gene) {
        this.chromosome[offset] = gene;
    }

    public int getGene(int offset) {
        return this.chromosome[offset];
    }

    public void setFitness(double fitness) {
        this.fitness = fitness;
    }

    public double getFitness() {
        return this.fitness;
    }

    public String toString() {
        String output = "";
        for (int gene = 0; gene < this.chromosome.length; gene++) {
            output += this.chromosome[gene];
        }
        return output;
    }
}
```

The Individual class represents a single candidate solution and is primarily responsible for storing and manipulating a chromosome. Note that the Individual class also has two constructors. One constructor accepts an integer (representing the length of the chromosome) and will create a random chromosome when initializing the object. The other constructor accepts an integer array and uses that as the chromosome.

Aside from managing the Individual's chromosome it also keeps track of the individual's fitness value, and also knows how to print itself as a string.

The next step is to create the Population class which provides the functionality needed to manage a group of individuals in a population.

As usual, comments and docblocks have been omitted from this chapter; be sure to look at the Eclipse project for more context!

```java
package chapter2;

import java.util.Arrays;
import java.util.Comparator;

public class Population {
        private Individual population[];
        private double populationFitness = -1;

        public Population(int populationSize) {
                this.population = new Individual[populationSize];
        }

        public Population(int populationSize, int chromosomeLength) {
                this.population = new Individual[populationSize];

                for (int individualCount = 0; individualCount <
                populationSize; individualCount++) {
                        Individual individual = new
                        Individual(chromosomeLength);
                        this.population[individualCount] = individual;
                }
        }

        public Individual[] getIndividuals() {
                return this.population;
        }
```

```java
    public Individual getFittest(int offset) {
        Arrays.sort(this.population, new Comparator<Individual>() {
            @Override
            public int compare(Individual o1, Individual o2) {
                if (o1.getFitness() > o2.getFitness()) {
                    return -1;
                } else if (o1.getFitness() < o2.getFitness()) {
                    return 1;
                }
                return 0;
            }
        });

        return this.population[offset];
    }

    public void setPopulationFitness(double fitness) {
        this.populationFitness = fitness;
    }

    public double getPopulationFitness() {
        return this.populationFitness;
    }

    public int size() {
        return this.population.length;
    }

    public Individual setIndividual(int offset, Individual individual) {
        return population[offset] = individual;
    }

        public Individual getIndividual(int offset) {
        return population[offset];
    }

    public void shuffle() {
        Random rnd = new Random();
        for (int i = population.length - 1; i > 0; i--) {
                int index = rnd.nextInt(i + 1);
                Individual a = population[index];
                population[index] = population[i];
                population[i] = a;
        }
    }
}
```

The population class is quite simple; its main function is to hold an array of individuals which can be accessed as needed in a convenient way by the class methods. Methods such as the getFittest() and setIndividual() are examples of methods which can access and update the individuals in the population. In addition to holding the individuals it also stores the population's total fitness which will become important later on when implementing the selection method.

Now that we have our population and individual classes, we can implement them in the GeneticAlgorithm class. To do so, simply create a method named 'initPopulatio' anywhere in the GeneticAlgorithm class.

```java
public class GeneticAlgorithm {
    /**
     * The constructor we created earlier is up here...
     */

    public Population initPopulation(int chromosomeLength) {
        Population population = new Population(this.populationSize,
            chromosomeLength);
        return population;
    }

    /**
     * We still have lots of methods to implement down here...
     */
}
```

Now that we have a Population and an Individual class, we can return to our 'AllOnesGA' class and start working with the 'initPopulation' method. Recall that the 'AllOnesGA' class only has a 'main' method, and that it represents the pseudocode presented earlier in the chapter.

When initializing the population in the main method, we also need to specify the length of individuals' chromosomes – here we are going to use a length of 50:

```java
public class AllOnesGA {
    public static void main(String[] args){
        // Create GA object
        GeneticAlgorithm ga = new GeneticAlgorithm(100, 0.01, 0.95, 0);

        // Initialize population
        Population population = ga.initPopulation(50);
    }
}
```

Evaluation

In the evaluation stage, each individual in the population has their fitness value calculated and stored for future use. To calculate the fitness of an individual we use a function known as the "fitness function".

Genetic algorithms operate by using *selection* to guide the evolutionary process towards better individuals. Because it's the fitness function that makes this selection possible, it's important that the fitness function is designed well and provides an accurate value for the individual's fitness. If the fitness function isn't well-designed it can take longer to find a solution which satisfies the minimum criteria, or possibly, fail to find an acceptable solution at all.

Fitness functions will often be the most computationally demanding components of a genetic algorithm. Because of this, it's important that the fitness function is also well optimized helping to prevent bottlenecks and allowing the algorithm to run efficiently.

Each specific optimization problem requires a uniquely developed fitness function. In our example of the all-ones problem, the fitness function is rather straightforward, simply counting the number of ones found within an individual's chromosome.

Now add a calcFitness method to the GeneticAlgorithm class. This method should count the number of ones in the chromosome, and then normalize the output to be between zero and one by dividing by the chromosome length. You may add this method anywhere in the GeneticAlgorithm class, so we've omitted the surrounding code below:

```
public double calcFitness(Individual individual) {

        // Track number of correct genes
        int correctGenes = 0;

        // Loop over individual's genes
        for (int geneIndex = 0; geneIndex < individual.getChromosomeLength();
        geneIndex++) {
                // Add one fitness point for each "1" found
                if (individual.getGene(geneIndex) == 1) {
                        correctGenes += 1;
                }
        }
```

```
    // Calculate fitness
    double fitness = (double) correctGenes / individual.
    getChromosomeLength();

    // Store fitness
    individual.setFitness(fitness);

    return fitness;
}
```

We also need a simple helper method to loop over every individual in the population and evaluate them (i.e., call calcFitness on each individual). Let's call this method evalPopulation and add it to the GeneticAlgorithm class as well. It should look like the following, and again you may add it anywhere:

```
public void evalPopulation(Population population) {
    double populationFitness = 0;

    for (Individual individual : population.getIndividuals()) {
        populationFitness += calcFitness(individual);
    }

    population.setPopulationFitness(populationFitness);
}
```

At this point, the GeneticAlgorithm class should have the following methods in it. For brevity's sake, we've omitted the body of the functions and are just showing a collapsed view of the class:

```
package chapter2;

public class GeneticAlgorithm {
    private int populationSize;
    private double mutationRate;
    private double crossoverRate;
    private int elitismCount;

    public GeneticAlgorithm(int populationSize, double mutationRate,
    double crossoverRate, int elitismCount) { }
    public Population initPopulation(int chromosomeLength) { }
    public double calcFitness(Individual individual) { }
    public void evalPopulation(Population population) { }
}
```

If you're missing any of these properties or methods, please go back and implement them now. We have four more methods to implement in the GeneticAlgorithm class: isTerminationConditionMet, selectParent, crossoverPopulation, and mutate Population.

Termination Check

The next thing needed is to check if our termination condition has been met. There are many different types of termination conditions. Sometimes, it's possible to know what the optimal solution is (rather, it's possible to know the fitness value of the optimal solution), in which case we can check directly for the correct solution. However, it's not always possible to know what the fitness of the best solution is, so we can terminate when the solution has become "good enough"; that is, whenever the solution exceeds some fitness threshold. We could also terminate when the algorithm has run for too long (too many generations), or we can combine a number of factors when deciding to terminate the algorithm.

Due to the simplicity of the all-ones problem, and the fact that we know the correct fitness should be 1, it's reasonable in this case to terminate when the correct solution has been found. This won't always be the case! In fact, it will only rarely be the case – but we're lucky this is an easy problem.

To begin, we must first construct a function which can check if our termination condition has occurred. We can do this by adding the following code to the GeneticAlgorithm class. Add this anywhere, and as usual we've omitted the surrounding class for brevity's sake.

```
public boolean isTerminationConditionMet(Population population) {
        for (Individual individual : population.getIndividuals()) {
                if (individual.getFitness() == 1) {
                        return true;
                }
        }

        return false;
}
```

The above method checks each individual in the population and will return true – indicating that we've found a termination condition and can stop – if the fitness of any individual in the population is 1.

Now that the termination condition has been built, a loop can be added to the main bootstrap method in the AllOnesGA class using the newly added termination check as its loop conditional. When the termination check returns true, the genetic algorithm will stop looping and return its results.

To create the evolution loop, modify the main method of our executive AllOnesGA class to represent the following. The first two lines of the snippet below are already in the main method. By adding this code we're continuing to implement the pseudocode presented at the beginning of the chapter – recall that the "main" method is a concrete representation of the genetic algorithm pseudocode. Here's what the main method should look like now:

```java
public static void main(String[] args) {
        // These two lines were already here:
        GeneticAlgorithm ga = new GeneticAlgorithm(100, 0.001, 0.95, 0);
        Population population = ga.initPopulation(50);

        // The following is the new code you should be adding:
        ga.evalPopulation(population);
        int generation = 1;

        while (ga.isTerminationConditionMet(population) == false) {
                // Print fittest individual from population
                System.out.println("Best solution: " + population.
                getFittest(0).toString());

                // Apply crossover
                // TODO!

                // Apply mutation
                // TODO!

                // Evaluate population
                ga.evalPopulation(population);

                // Increment the current generation
                generation++;
        }

        System.out.println("Found solution in " + generation + "
        generations");
        System.out.println("Best solution: " + population.getFittest(0).
        toString());
}
```

We've added an evolution loop that checks the output of isTerminationConditionMet. Also new to the main method are the addition of evalPopulation calls both before and during the loop, the generation variable that keeps track of the generation number, and the debug message that helpfully lets you know what the best solution in each generation looks like.

We've also added an end-game: when we exit the loop, we'll print some information about the final solution.

However, at this point our genetic algorithm will *run*, but it won't ever evolve! We'll be stuck in an infinite loop unless we're lucky enough that one of our randomly generated individuals happens to be all ones. You can see this behavior directly by clicking the "Run" button in Eclipse; the same solution will be presented over and over and the loop will never end. You'll have to force the program to stop running by clicking the "Terminate" button above Eclipse's console.

To continue building our genetic algorithm we need to implement two additional concepts: crossover and mutation. These concepts actually drive the evolution of a population forward through random mutation and survival of the fittest.

Crossover

At this point, it's time to start evolving the population by applying mutation and crossover. The crossover operator is the process in which individuals from the population trade genetic information, hopefully to create a new individual which contains the best parts from its parents' genomes.

During crossover each individual in the population is considered for crossover; this is where the crossover rate parameter is used. By comparing the crossover rate to a random number, we can decide whether the individual should have crossover applied to it, or whether it should be added straight into the next population unaffected by crossover. If an individual is selected for crossover then a second parent needs be found. To find the second parent, we need to pick one of many possible selection methods.

Roulette Wheel Selection

Roulette wheel selection - also known as fitness proportionate selection - is a selection method which uses the analogy of a roulette wheel to select individuals from a population. The idea is that individuals from the population are placed on a metaphoric roulette wheel depending on their fitness value. The higher the fitness of the individual, the more space it's allocated on the roulette wheel. The image below demonstrates how individuals are typically positioned in this process.

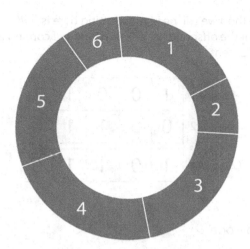

Each number on the wheel above represents an individual from the population. The higher the fitness of the individual, the larger their portion of the roulette wheel. If you now imagine spinning this wheel, it's much more likely that the fitter individuals will be picked because they fill more space on the wheel. This is why this selection method is often referred to as fitness proportionate selection; because solutions are selected based on their fitness in proportion to the fitness of the rest of the population.

There are many other selection methods that we could use such as: tournament selection (Chapter 3) and stochastic universal sampling (an advanced form of fitness proportional selection). However, in this chapter we will be implementing one of the most common selection methods: roulette wheel selection. In later chapters we will be looking at other selection methods and how they differ.

Crossover Methods

In addition to the various selection methods that can be used during crossover, there are also different methods to exchange the genetic information between two individuals. Different problems have slightly different properties and work better with specific crossover methods. For example, the all-ones problem simply requires a string that consists entirely of 1s. A string of "00111" has the same fitness value as a string of "10101" – they both contain three 1s. With genetic algorithms of this type, this isn't always the case. Imagine we are trying to create a string which lists, in order, the numbers one to five. In this case the string "12345" has a very different fitness value from "52431". This is because we're not just looking for the correct numbers, but also the correct order. For problems such as this, a crossover method that respects the order of the genes is preferable.

The crossover method we will be implementing here is *uniform crossover*. In this method each gene of the offspring has a 50% change of coming from either its first parent or its second parent.

Parent 1	1	0	0	1	1
Parent 2	0	0	1	1	0
Offspring	1	0	1	1	0

Crossover Pseudo Code

Now that we have a selection and a crossover method, let's look at some pseudo code which outlines the crossover process to be implemented.

```
1: For each individual in population:
2:      newPopulation = new array;
2:         If crossoverRate > random():
3:              secondParent = selectParent();
4:              offspring = crossover(individual, secondParent);
5:              newPopulation.push(offspring);
6:         Else:
7:              newPopulation.push(individual);
8:         End if
9: End loop;
```

Crossover Implementation

To implement roulette wheel selection, add a selectParent() method anywhere in the GeneticAlgorithm class.

```
public Individual selectParent(Population population) {
        // Get individuals
        Individual individuals[] = population.getIndividuals();

        // Spin roulette wheel
        double populationFitness = population.getPopulationFitness();
        double rouletteWheelPosition = Math.random() * populationFitness;
```

```
        // Find parent
        double spinWheel = 0;
        for (Individual individual : individuals) {
                spinWheel += individual.getFitness();
                if (spinWheel >= rouletteWheelPosition) {
                        return individual;
                }
        }
        return individuals[population.size() - 1];
}
```

The selectParent() method essentially runs a roulette wheel in reverse; at a casino, the wheel already has markings on it, and then you spin the wheel and wait for the ball to drop into position. Here, however, we select a random position *first* and then work backward to figure out which individual lies in that position. Algorithmically, it's easier this way. Choose a random number between 0 and the total population fitness, then loop through each individual, summing their fitnesses as you go, until you reach the random position you chose at the outset.

Now that the selection method has been added, the next step is to create the crossover method using this selectParent() method to select the crossover mates. To begin, add the following crossover method to the GeneticAlgorithm class.

```
public Population crossoverPopulation(Population population) {
        // Create new population
        Population newPopulation = new Population(population.size());

        // Loop over current population by fitness
        for (int populationIndex = 0; populationIndex < population.size();
        populationIndex++) {
                Individual parent1 = population.getFittest(populationIndex);

                // Apply crossover to this individual?
                if (this.crossoverRate > Math.random() && populationIndex >
                this.elitismCount) {
                        // Initialize offspring
                        Individual offspring = new Individual(parent1.
                        getChromosomeLength());

                        // Find second parent
                        Individual parent2 = selectParent(population);

                        // Loop over genome
                        for (int geneIndex = 0; geneIndex < parent1.
                        getChromosomeLength(); geneIndex++) {
                                // Use half of parent1's genes and half of
                                parent2's genes
```

```
                    if (0.5 > Math.random()) {
                        offspring.setGene(geneIndex,
                        parent1.getGene(geneIndex));
                    } else {
                        offspring.setGene(geneIndex,
                        parent2.getGene(geneIndex));
                    }
                }

                // Add offspring to new population
                newPopulation.setIndividual(populationIndex,
                offspring);
            } else {
                // Add individual to new population without applying
                crossover
                newPopulation.setIndividual
                (populationIndex, parent1);
            }
        }

    return newPopulation;
}
```

In the first line of the crossoverPopulation() method, a new empty population is created for the next generation. Next, the population is looped over and the crossover rate is used to consider each individual for crossover. (There's also a mysterious "elitism" term here, which we'll discuss in the next section.) If the individual doesn't go through crossover, its added straight to the next population, otherwise a new individual is created. The offspring's chromosome is filled by looping over the parent chromosomes and randomly adding genes from each parent to the offspring's chromosome. When this crossover process has finished for each individual of the population, the crossover method returns the next generation's population.

From here we can implement the crossover function into our main method in the AllOnesGA class. The entire AllOnesGA class and main method is printed below; however the only change from before is the addition of the line that calls crossoverPopulation() below the "Apply crossover" comment.

```
package chapter2;
public class AllOnesGA {
    public static void main(String[] args) {
        // Create GA object
        GeneticAlgorithm ga = new GeneticAlgorithm(100, 0.001, 0.95, 0);

        // Initialize population
        Population population = ga.initPopulation(50);
```

```
        // Evaluate population
        ga.evalPopulation(population);

        // Keep track of current generation
        int generation = 1;

        while (ga.isTerminationConditionMet(population) == false) {
            // Print fittest individual from population
            System.out.println("Best solution: " + population.
            getFittest(0).toString());

            // Apply crossover
            population = ga.crossoverPopulation(population);

            // Apply mutation
            // TODO

            // Evaluate population
            ga.evalPopulation(population);

            // Increment the current generation
            generation++;
        }

        System.out.println("Found solution in " + generation + "
        generations");
        System.out.println("Best solution: " + population.
        getFittest(0).toString());
    }
}
```

At this point, running the program should work and return a valid solution! Try it for yourself by clicking the Run button in Eclipse and observing the console that appears.

As you can see, crossover alone is sufficient to evolve a population. However, genetic algorithms without mutation are prone to getting stuck in local optima without ever finding the global optimum. We won't see this demonstrated in such a simple problem, but in more complex problem domains we need some mechanism to nudge a population away from local optimums to try and see if there's a better solution elsewhere. This is where the randomness of mutation comes into play: if a solution is stagnating near a local optimum, a random event may kick it in the right direction and send it toward a better solution.

Elitism

Before discussing mutation, let's take a look at the "elitismCount" parameter we introduced in the crossover method.

A basic genetic algorithm will often lose the best individuals in a population between generations due to the effects of the crossover and mutation operators. However, we need these operators to find better solutions. To see this problem in action, simply edit your genetic algorithm's code to print the fitness of the fittest individual over each generation. You'll notice that although it will typically go up, there are occasions when the fittest solution is lost and replaced with a less optimal one during crossover and mutation.

One simple optimization technique used to tackle this problem is to always allow the fittest individual, or individuals, to be added unaltered to the next generation's population. This way the best individuals are no longer lost from generation to generation. Although these individuals don't have crossover applied to them, they can still be selected as a parent for another individual allowing their genetic information to still be shared with others in the population. This process of retaining the best for the next generation is called *elitism*.

Typically, the optimal number of 'elite' individuals in a population will be a very small proportion of the total population size. This is because if the value is too high, it will slow down the genetic algorithm's search process due to a lack of genetic diversity caused by preserving too many individuals. Similarly to the other parameters discussed previously, it's important to find a balance for optimal performance.

Implementing elitism is simple in both crossover and mutation contexts. Let's revisit the conditional in crossoverPopulation() that checks to see if crossover should be applied:

```
// Apply crossover to this individual?
if (this.crossoverRate > Math.random() && populationIndex >= this.
elitismCount) {
    // ...
}
```

Crossover is only applied if *both* the crossover conditional is met *and* the individual is not considered elite.

What makes an individual elite? At this point, the individuals in the population have already been sorted by their fitness, so the strongest individuals have the lowest indices. Therefore, if we want three elite individuals, we should skip indices 0-2 from consideration. This will preserve the strongest individuals and let them pass through to the next generation unmodified. We'll use the same exact conditional in the mutation code to follow.

Mutation

The last thing we need to add to complete the evolution process is *mutation*. Like crossover, there are many different mutation methods to choose from. When using binary strings one of the more common methods is called *bit flip mutation*. As you may have guessed, bit flip mutation involves flipping the value of the bit from 1 to 0, or from 0 to 1, depending on its initial value. When the chromosome is encoded using some other representation, a different mutation method would usually be implemented to make better use of the encoding.

One of the most important factors in selecting mutation and crossover methods is to make sure that the method you've selected still yields a valid solution. We'll see this concept in action in later chapters, but for this problem we simply need to make sure that 0 and 1 are the only possible values a gene can mutate to. A gene mutating to, say, 7 would give us an invalid solution.

This advice seems moot and over-obvious in this chapter, but consider a different simple problem where you need to order the numbers one through six without repeating (i.e., end up with "123456"). A mutation algorithm that simply chose a random number between one and six could yield "126456", using "6" twice, which would be an invalid solution because each number can only be used once. As you can see, even simple problems sometimes require sophisticated techniques.

Similarly to crossover, mutation is applied to the individual based on the mutation rate. If the mutation rate is set to 0.1 then each gene has a 10% chance of being mutated during the mutation stage.

Let's go ahead and add the mutation function to our GeneticAlgorithm class. We can add this anywhere:

```
public Population mutatePopulation(Population population) {
        // Initialize new population
        Population newPopulation = new Population(this.populationSize);

        // Loop over current population by fitness
        for (int populationIndex = 0; populationIndex < population.size();
populationIndex++) {
                Individual individual = population.
                getFittest(populationIndex);

                // Loop over individual's genes
                for (int geneIndex = 0; geneIndex < individual.
getChromosomeLength(); geneIndex++) {
                        // Skip mutation if this is an elite individual
                        if (populationIndex >= this.elitismCount) {
                                // Does this gene need mutation?
                                if (this.mutationRate > Math.random()) {
                                        // Get new gene
                                        int newGene = 1;
```

```
                                    if (individual.getGene(geneIndex) == 1) {
                                        newGene = 0;
                                    }
                                    // Mutate gene
                                    individual.setGene(geneIndex, newGene);
                            }
                        }
                    }

                    // Add individual to population
                    newPopulation.setIndividual(populationIndex, individual);
            }

            // Return mutated population
            return newPopulation;
    }
```

The mutatePopulation() method starts by creating a new empty population for the mutated individuals and then begins to loop over the current population. Each individual's chromosome is then looped over and each gene is considered for bit flip mutation using the mutation rate. When the entire chromosome of an individual has been looped over, the individual is then added to the new mutation population. When all individuals have gone through the mutation process the mutated population is returned.

Now we can complete the final step of the evolution loop by adding the mutate function to the main method. The finished main method is as follows. There are only two differences from the last time: first, we've added the call to mutatePopulation() below the "Apply mutation" comment. Also, we've changed the "elitismCount" parameter in the "new GeneticAlgorithm" constructor from 0 to 2, now that we understand how elitism works.

```
package chapter2;
public class AllOnesGA {

        public static void main(String[] args) {
                // Create GA object
                GeneticAlgorithm ga = new GeneticAlgorithm(100, 0.001, 0.95, 2);

                // Initialize population
                Population population = ga.initPopulation(50);

                // Evaluate population
                ga.evalPopulation(population);

                // Keep track of current generation
                int generation = 1;
```

```
        while (ga.isTerminationConditionMet(population) == false) {
            // Print fittest individual from population
            System.out.println("Best solution: " + population.
            getFittest(0).toString());

            // Apply crossover
            population = ga.crossoverPopulation(population);

            // Apply mutation
            population = ga.mutatePopulation(population);

            // Evaluate population
            ga.evalPopulation(population);

            // Increment the current generation
            generation++;
        }

        System.out.println("Found solution in " + generation + "
        generations");
        System.out.println("Best solution: " + population.
        getFittest(0).toString());
    }
}
```

Execution

You've now completed your first genetic algorithm. The Individual and Population classes are printed in their entirety earlier in the chapter, and your version of those classes should look exactly like the above. The final AllOnesGA executive class–the class that bootstraps and runs the algorithm–is provided directly above.

The GeneticAlgorithm class is quite long, and you built it piece by piece, so at this point please check that you've implemented the following properties and methods. To save space I've omitted all comments and method bodies here—I'm just showing a collapsed view of the class–but make sure your version of the class has each one of these methods implemented as described above.

```
package chapter2;

public class GeneticAlgorithm {
    private int populationSize;
    private double mutationRate;
    private double crossoverRate;
    private int elitismCount;

    public GeneticAlgorithm(int populationSize, double mutationRate, double
```

```
        crossoverRate, int elitismCount) { }
    public Population initPopulation(int chromosomeLength) { }
    public double calcFitness(Individual individual) { }
    public void evalPopulation(Population population) { }
    public boolean isTerminationConditionMet(Population population) { }
    public Individual selectParent(Population population) { }
    public Population crossoverPopulation(Population population) { }
    public Population mutatePopulation(Population population) { }
}
```

If you're using the Eclipse IDE, you can now run the algorithm by opening up the AllOnesGA file and clicking the "Run" button, found typically in the top menu of the IDE.

While running, the algorithm will print information to the console, which should automatically appear in Eclipse when clicking Run. Because of the randomness of every genetic algorithm, each run will look a little bit different, but here's an example of what your output may look like:

```
Best solution: 110011101001101111110101110010011001111110011111111
Best solution: 110011101001101111110101110010011001111110011111111
Best solution: 110011101001101111110101110010011001111110011111111
[ ... Lots of lines omitted here ... ]
Best solution: 111111111111111111111111111111011111111111111111111
Best solution: 111111111111111111111111111111011111111111111111111
Found solution in 113 generations
Best solution: 111111111111111111111111111111111111111111111111111
```

At this point, you should play with the various parameters you've given to the GeneticAlgorithm constructor: populationSize, mutationRate, crossoverRate, and elitismCount. Don't forget that statistics rule the performance of genetic algorithms, so you can't evaluate the performance of an algorithm or a setting with only one run – you'll want to run at least 10 trials of each different setting before judging its performance.

Summary

In this chapter, you've learned the basics of implementing a genetic algorithm. The pseudocode at the beginning of the chapter provides a generic conceptual model for all genetic algorithms you'll implement throughout the rest of the book: each genetic algorithm will initialize and evaluate a population, and then enter a loop that performs crossover, mutation, and re-evaluation. The loop only exits if a termination condition is met.

Throughout this chapter you built the supporting components of a genetic algorithm, particularly the Individual and Population classes, which you'll largely reuse in the following chapters. You then purpose-built a GeneticAlgorithm class to solve the "all ones" problem specifically, and ran it successfully.

You've also learned the following: while each genetic algorithm is similar conceptually and structurally, different problem domains will require different implementations of evaluation techniques (i.e., fitness scoring, crossover techniques, and mutation techniques).

The rest of this book will explore those different techniques through example problems. In the following chapters you'll reuse the Population and Individual classes with only slight modifications. However, each following chapter will require heavy modifications to the GeneticAlgorithm class, as that class is where crossover, mutation, termination conditions, and fitness evaluation occurs.

EXERCISES

1. Run the genetic algorithm a few times observing the randomness of the evolutionary process. How many generations does it typically take to find a solution to this problem?

2. Increase and decrease the population size. How does decreasing the population size affect the speed of the algorithm and does it also affect the number of generations it takes to find a solution? How does increasing the population size affect the speed of the algorithm and how does it affect the number of generations it takes to find a solution?

3. Set the mutation rate to 0. How does this affect the genetic algorithms ability to find a solution? Use a high mutation rate, how does this affect the algorithm?

4. Apply a low crossover rate. How does the algorithm preform with a lower crossover rate?

5. Decrease and increase the complexity of the problem by experimenting with shorter and larger chromosomes. Do different parameters work better when dealing with shorter or larger chromosomes?

6. Compare the genetic algorithm's performance with and without elitism enabled.

7. Run tests using high elitism values. How does this affect the search performance?

EXERCISES

Chapter 3

Introduction

In this chapter, we are going to use the knowledge we gained from the previous chapter to solve a real world problem using a genetic algorithm. The real world problem we will be working on is designing robotic controllers.

Genetic algorithms are often applied to robotics as a method of designing sophisticated robotic controllers that enable a robot to perform complex tasks and behaviors, removing the need to manually code a complicated robotic controller. Imagine you have built a robot that can transport goods around a warehouse. You have installed sensors, which allow the robot to see its local environment, and you have given it wheels so it can navigate based on input from its sensors. The problem is how you can link the sensor data to motor actions so that the robot can navigate the warehouse.

The field of artificial intelligence where genetic algorithms, and more generally, the ideas of Darwinian evolution are applied to robotics is referred to as *evolutionary robotics*. This isn't the only bottom-up approach used for this problem, however. Neural networks are also frequently used to successfully map robotic sensors to outputs by using reinforcement-learning algorithms to guide the learning process.

Typically, a genetic algorithm will evaluate a large population of individuals to locate the best individuals for the next generation. Evaluating an individual is done by running a fitness function that gauges the performance of an individual based on certain pre-defined criteria. However, applying genetic algorithms and their fitness functions to physical robots gives rise to a new challenge; physically evaluating each robotic controller isn't feasible for large populations. This is due to the difficulty in physically testing each robotic controller and the time it would take to do so. For this reason, robotic controllers are typically evaluated by applying them to simulated models of real, physical robots and environments. This enables quick evaluations of each controller in software that later can be applied to their physical counterparts. In this chapter, we will use our knowledge of binary genetic algorithms to design a robotic controller and begin applying it to a virtual robot in a virtual environment.

The Problem

The problem we are going to solve is designing a robotic controller that can use the robots sensors to navigate a robot successfully through a maze. The robot can take four actions: move one-step forward, turn left, turn right, or, rarely, do nothing. The robot also has six sensors: three on the front, one on the left, one on the right and one on the back.

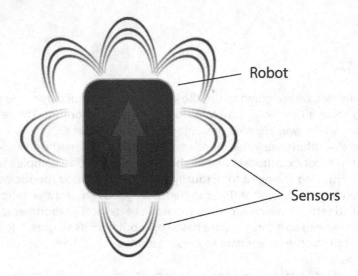

The maze we are going to explore is comprised of walls that the robot can't cross and will have an outlined route, shown in Figure 3-1, which we want the robot to follow. Keep in mind that the purpose of this chapter isn't to train a robot to solve mazes. Our purpose is to automatically program a robot controller with six sensors so that it doesn't crash into walls; we're simply using the maze as a complicated environment in which to test our robot controller.

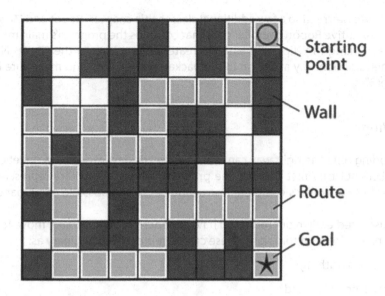

Figure 3-1. The route we want the robot to follow

The robot's sensors will activate whenever they detect a wall adjacent to the sensor. For example, the robot's front sensor will activate if it detects a wall in front of the robot.

Implementation

Before You Start

This chapter will build on the code you developed in Chapter 2. Before you start, create a new Eclipse or NetBeans project, or create a new package in your existing project for this book called "chapter3".

Copy the Individual, Population, and GeneticAlgorithm classes over from Chapter 2 and import them into chapter 3. Make sure to update the package name at the top of each class file! They should all say "package chapter3" at the very top.

In this chapter, you won't have to modify the Individual and Population classes at all, except for changing the package name to "chapter3".

However, you will be modifying several methods in the GeneticAlgorithm class. At this point, you should completely delete the following five methods: calcFitness, evalPopulation, isTerminationConditionMet, selectParent, and crossoverPopulation. You'll rewrite these five methods throughout this chapter, and deleting them right now will help ensure you don't accidentally reuse Chapter 2's implementations.

You'll also be creating a few additional classes this chapter (Robot and Maze, and also the executive RobotController class that contains the program's main method). If you're working in Eclipse, it's easy to create a new class via the File ➤ New ➤ Class menu option. Pay attention to the package name field and make sure it says "chapter3".

Encoding

Encoding data the right way can often be the trickiest aspect of a genetic algorithm. Let's start by first defining the problem: we need a binary representation of the robot controller's complete instruction set for all possible combinations of inputs.

As discussed earlier, our robot will have four actions: do nothing, move forward one step, turn left and turn right. These can be represented in binary as:

- "00": do nothing
- "01": move forward
- "10": turn left
- "11": turn right

We also have six different on/off sensors giving us 2^6 (64) possible combinations of sensor inputs. If each action requires 2 bits to encode, we can represent the controller's response to *any possible input* in 128 bits. Phrased another way, we have 64 different scenarios our robot can find itself in, and our controller needs to have an action defined for each scenario. Since an action requires two bits, our controller requires 64*2 = 128 bits of storage.

Since genetic algorithm chromosomes are easiest to manipulate as arrays, our chromosome will be a bit array of length 128. In this scenario, with our mutation and crossover methods you don't need to worry about which particular instruction they're modifying, they just get to manipulate genetic code. On our end, however, we'll have to unpack the encoded data before we can use it in the robot controller.

Given that 128 bits is our requirement for representing instructions for 64 different sensor combinations, how should we actually *structure* the chromosome so that we can pack and unpack it? That is, which combination of sensor inputs does each section of the chromosome correspond to? In what *order* are the actions? Where can we find the action for the situation "front and front-right sensors are activated" within the chromosome? The bits in the chromosome represent *output*, but how is *input* represented?

This will be an unintuitive question (and solution) to many people, so let's move toward the solution in small steps. The first step might be to consider a simple, human readable list of inputs and outputs:

```
Sensor #1 (front): on
Sensor #2 (front-left): off
Sensor #3 (front-right): on
Sensor #4 (left): off
Sensor #5 (right): off
Sensor #6 (back): off
```

Instruction: turn left (action "10" as defined above)

With an additional 63 entries to represent all possible combinations, this format is unwieldy. It's clear that this type of enumeration won't work for us. Let's take another small step by abbreviating everything and translating "on" and "off" to 1 and 0:

```
#1: 1
#2: 0
#3: 1
#4: 0
#5: 0
#6: 0
```

Instruction: 10

We're making progress, but this still doesn't pack 64 instructions into a 128-bit array. Our next step is to take the six sensor values – the inputs – and encode those further. Let's line them up from right to left, and drop the word "Instruction" from the output:

```
#6:0, #5:0, #4:0, #3:1, #2:0, #1:1 => 10
```

Now let's drop the numbering of the sensors:

```
000101 => 10
```

If we now convert the sensor values' bit string to decimal, we get the following:

```
5 => 10
```

Now we're onto something. The "5" on the left hand side represents the sensor inputs, and the "10" on the right represents what the robot should do when faced with those inputs (the output). Because we got here from a binary representation of the sensor inputs, there's *only one combination* of sensors that can give us the number 5.

We can use the number 5 as the *position* in the chromosome that represents a combination of sensor inputs. If we were building this chromosome by hand, and we knew that "10" (turn left) is the correct response to "5" (front and front-right sensors detecting a wall), we would place "1" and "0" in the 11th and 12th spots in the chromosome (each action requires 2 bits, and we start counting positions from 0), like so:

```
xx xx xx xx xx 10 xx xx xx xx (... 54 more pairs...)
```

In the above fake chromosome, the first pair (position 0) represents the action to take when the sensor inputs total is 0: everything off. The second pair (position 1) represents the action to take when the sensor inputs total 1: only the front sensor detects a wall. The third pair, position 2, represents only the front-left sensor triggered. The fourth pair, position 3, represents both the front and the front-left sensor being active. And so on, until you get to the final pair, position 63, which represents all sensors being triggered.

Another visualization of this encoding scheme is represented in Figure 3-2. The left-most "Sensors" column represents the sensors' bitfield, which maps to a chromosome position after you convert the bitfield to decimal. Once you've converted the sensors' bitfield to decimal, you can place the desired action at the corresponding location in the chromosome.

Sensors						Action	Chromosome
B	R	L	FR	FL	F		
0	0	0	0	0	0	11	**11**001001101001...11
0	0	0	0	0	1	00	11**00**1001101001...11
0	0	0	0	1	0	10	1100**10**01101001...11
0	0	0	0	1	1	01	110010**01**101001...11
0	0	0	1	0	0	10	11001001**10**1001...11
0	0	0	1	0	1	10	1100100110**10**01...11
0	0	0	1	1	0	01	110010011010**01**...11
1	1	1	1	1	1	11	11001001101001...**11**

Figure 3-2. Mapping the sensor values to actions

This encoding scheme may seem obtuse at first – and the chromosome is not human-readable – but it has a couple of helpful properties. First, the chromosome can be manipulated as an array of bits, rather than a complicated tree structure or hashmap, which makes crossover, mutation and other manipulations much easier. Secondly, every 128-bit value is a valid solution (though not necessarily a good one) – more on this later in the chapter.

Figure 3-2 describes how a typical chromosome can map the robot's sensor values to actions.

Initialization

In this implementation, we first need to create and initialize a maze to run the robot in. To do this, create the following Maze class to manage the maze. This can be done with the following code. Create a new class in Eclipse by selecting File ➤ New ➤ Class, and make sure to use the correct package name, especially if you've copied files over from Chapter 2.

```java
package chapter3;

import java.util.ArrayList;

public class Maze {
    private final int maze[][];
    private int startPosition[] = { -1, -1 };

    public Maze(int maze[][]) {
        this.maze = maze;
    }

    public int[] getStartPosition() {
        // Check if we've already found start position
        if (this.startPosition[0] != -1 && this.startPosition[1] != -1) {
            return this.startPosition;
        }

        // Default return value
        int startPosition[] = { 0, 0 };

        // Loop over rows
        for (int rowIndex = 0; rowIndex < this.maze.length;
        rowIndex++) {
            // Loop over columns
            for (int colIndex = 0; colIndex < this.maze[rowIndex].
            length; colIndex++) {
                // 2 is the type for start position
```

```
                          if (this.maze[rowIndex][colIndex] == 2) {
                              this.startPosition = new int[] {
                              colIndex, rowIndex };
                              return new int[] { colIndex, rowIndex };
                          }
                      }
                  }

        return startPosition;
    }

    public int getPositionValue(int x, int y) {
        if (x < 0 || y < 0 || x >= this.maze.length || y >=
        this.maze[0].length) {
            return 1;
        }
        return this.maze[y][x];
    }

    public boolean isWall(int x, int y) {
        return (this.getPositionValue(x, y) == 1);
    }

    public int getMaxX() {
        return this.maze[0].length - 1;
    }

    public int getMaxY() {
        return this.maze.length - 1;
    }

    public int scoreRoute(ArrayList<int[]> route) {
        int score = 0;
        boolean visited[][] = new boolean[this.getMaxY() + 1]
        [this.getMaxX() + 1];

        // Loop over route and score each move
        for (Object routeStep : route) {
            int step[] = (int[]) routeStep;
            if (this.maze[step[1]][step[0]] == 3 &&
            visited[step[1]][step[0]] == false) {
                // Increase score for correct move
                score++;
                // Remove reward
                visited[step[1]][step[0]] = true;
            }
        }
```

```
        return score;
    }
}
```

This code contains a constructor to create a new maze from a double int array and public methods to get the start position, check a position's value and score a route through the maze.

The scoreRoute method is the most significant method in the Maze class; it evaluates a route taken by the robot and returns a fitness score based on the number of correct tiles it stepped on. The score returned by this scoreRoute method is what we'll use as the individual's fitness score in the GeneticAlgorithm class' calcFitness method later.

Now that we have a maze abstraction, we can create our executive class – the class that actually executes the algorithm – and initialize the maze that was shown in Figure 3-1. Create another new class called RobotController, and create the "main" method that the program will boot from.

```java
package chapter3;

public class RobotController {

    public static int maxGenerations = 1000;

    public static void main(String[] args) {

        /**
         * 0 = Empty
         * 1 = Wall
         * 2 = Starting position
         * 3 = Route
         * 4 = Goal position
         */

        Maze maze = new Maze(new int[][] {
            { 0, 0, 0, 0, 1, 0, 1, 3, 2 },
            { 1, 0, 1, 1, 1, 0, 1, 3, 1 },
            { 1, 0, 0, 1, 3, 3, 3, 3, 1 },
            { 3, 3, 3, 1, 3, 1, 1, 0, 1 },
            { 3, 1, 3, 3, 3, 1, 1, 0, 0 },
            { 3, 3, 1, 1, 1, 1, 0, 1, 1 },
            { 1, 3, 0, 1, 3, 3, 3, 3, 3 },
            { 0, 3, 1, 1, 3, 1, 0, 1, 3 },
            { 1, 3, 3, 3, 3, 1, 1, 1, 4 }
        });
```

```
    /**
     * We'll implement the genetic algorithm pseudocode
     * from chapter 2 here....
     */

    }
}
```

The maze object we've created uses integers to represent different terrain types: 1 defines a wall; 2 is the starting position, 3 traces the best route through the maze, 4 is the goal position and 0 is an empty position that the robot can travel over but isn't on the route to the goal.

Next, similarly to our previous implementation, we need to initialize a population of random individuals. Each of these individuals should have a chromosome length of 128. As explained earlier, 128 bits allows for us to map all 64 inputs to an action. Since it's not possible to create an invalid chromosome for this problem, we can use the same random initialization as before – recall that this random initialization occurs in the Individual class constructor, which we copied un-modified from Chapter 2. A robot initialized in such a manner will simply take random actions when presented with different situations, and through generations of evolution, we hope to refine this behavior.

Before stubbing out the familiar genetic algorithm pseudocode from Chapter 2 in our main method, we should make one modification to the GeneticAlgorithm class that we copied from Chapter 2. We're going to add a property called "tournamentSize" – which we'll discuss in depth later in this chapter – to the GeneticAlgorithm class and constructor.

Modify the top of your GeneticAlgorithm class to look like this:

```
package chapter3;
public class GeneticAlgorithm {

    /**
     * See chapter2/GeneticAlgorithm for a description of these
       properties.
     */
    private int populationSize;
    private double mutationRate;
    private double crossoverRate;
    private int elitismCount;

    /**
     * A new property we've introduced is the size of the population
       used for
     * tournament selection in crossover.
     */
```

```
    protected int tournamentSize;

    public GeneticAlgorithm(int populationSize, double mutationRate,
    double crossoverRate, int elitismCount,
                int tournamentSize) {

        this.populationSize = populationSize;
        this.mutationRate = mutationRate;
        this.crossoverRate = crossoverRate;
        this.elitismCount = elitismCount;
        this.tournamentSize = tournamentSize;
    }

    /**
     * We're not going to show the rest of the class here,
     * but methods like initPopulation, mutatePopulation,
     * and evaluatePopulation should appear below.
     */
}
```

We've made three simple changes: first, we've added "protected int tournamentSize" to the class properties. Second, we've added "int tournamentSize" as the fifth argument to the constructor. Finally, we've added the "this.tournament Size = tournamentSize" assignment to the constructor.

With the tournamentSize property handled, we can move forward and stub out our pseudocode from Chapter 2. As always, this code will go in the "main" method of the executive class, which in this case we named RobotController.

The code below won't do anything, of course – we haven't implemented any of the methods we need yet and have replaced everything with TODO comments. But stubbing the main method out in this manner helps to reinforce the conceptual execution model of a genetic algorithm, and also helps us keep on track in terms of methods we still need to implement; there are seven TODOs in this class that need to be resolved.

Update your RobotController class to look like the following. The maze definition is the same as before, but everything below it is a new addition to this file.

```
package chapter3;

public class RobotController {

    public static int maxGenerations = 1000;

    public static void main(String[] args) {
```

```
Maze maze = new Maze(new int[][] {
        { 0, 0, 0, 0, 1, 0, 1, 3, 2 },
        { 1, 0, 1, 1, 1, 0, 1, 3, 1 },
        { 1, 0, 0, 1, 3, 3, 3, 3, 1 },
        { 3, 3, 3, 1, 3, 1, 1, 0, 1 },
        { 3, 1, 3, 3, 3, 1, 1, 0, 0 },
        { 3, 3, 1, 1, 1, 1, 0, 1, 1 },
        { 1, 3, 0, 1, 3, 3, 3, 3, 3 },
        { 0, 3, 1, 1, 3, 1, 0, 1, 3 },
        { 1, 3, 3, 3, 3, 1, 1, 1, 4 }
});

// Create genetic algorithm
GeneticAlgorithm ga = new GeneticAlgorithm(200, 0.05,
0.9, 2, 10);
Population population = ga.initPopulation(128);

// TODO: Evaluate population

int generation = 1;

// Start evolution loop
while (/* TODO */ false) {
        // TODO: Print fittest individual from population

        // TODO: Apply crossover

        // TODO: Apply mutation

        // TODO: Evaluate population

        // Increment the current generation
        generation++;
}
// TODO: Print results

    }
}
```

There are only slight differences between this RobotController class and the AllOnesGA class from Chapter 2. The AllOnesGA class didn't have the "maxGenerations" property, because we knew exactly what the target fitness score was. In this case, however, we'll learn about a different way to end the evolution loop. The AllOnesGA class didn't need a Maze class either, but you'll often find supporting classes like Maze in real genetic algorithm problems. Additionally, this version of the GeneticAlgorithm class takes 5 parameters, not 4, because we're expecting to introduce a new concept called "tournament selection" in this chapter. Finally, the chromosome length in this example is 128 as opposed to 50 as in Chapter 2. In the last chapter, the chromosome length was arbitrary, but in this case, the chromosome length is meaningful and dictated by the encoding method discussed earlier.

Evaluation

In the evaluation phase, we need to define a fitness function that can evaluate each robotic controller. We can do this by increasing the individual's fitness for each correct unique move made on the route. Recall that the Maze class we created earlier has a scoreRoute method that performs this evaluation. However, the route itself comes from a robot under autonomous control. So, before we can give the Maze class a route to evaluate, we need to create a Robot that can follow instructions and generate a route by executing those instructions.

Create a Robot class to manage the robot's functionality. In Eclipse, you can create a new class by selecting the menu option File ➤ New ➤ Class. Make sure to use the correct package name. Add this code to the file:

```java
package chapter3;
import java.util.ArrayList;

/**
 * A robot abstraction. Give it a maze and an instruction set, and it will
 * attempt to navigate to the finish.
 *
 * @author bkanber
 *
 */
public class Robot {
    private enum Direction {NORTH, EAST, SOUTH, WEST};

    private int xPosition;
    private int yPosition;
    private Direction heading;
    int maxMoves;
    int moves;
    private int sensorVal;
    private final int sensorActions[];
    private Maze maze;
    private ArrayList<int[]> route;
```

```java
/**
 * Initalize a robot with controller
 *
 * @param sensorActions The string to map the sensor value to actions
 * @param maze The maze the robot will use
 * @param maxMoves The maximum number of moves the robot can make
 */
public Robot(int[] sensorActions, Maze maze, int maxMoves){
    this.sensorActions = this.calcSensorActions(sensorActions);
    this.maze = maze;
    int startPos[] = this.maze.getStartPosition();
    this.xPosition = startPos[0];
    this.yPosition = startPos[1];
    this.sensorVal = -1;
    this.heading = Direction.EAST;
    this.maxMoves = maxMoves;
    this.moves = 0;
    this.route = new ArrayList<int[]>();
    this.route.add(startPos);
}

/**
 * Runs the robot's actions based on sensor inputs
 */
public void run(){
    while(true){
        this.moves++;

        // Break if the robot stops moving
        if (this.getNextAction() == 0) {
            return;
        }

        // Break if we reach the goal
        if (this.maze.getPositionValue(this.xPosition,
        this.yPosition) == 4) {
            return;
        }

        // Break if we reach a maximum number of moves
        if (this.moves > this.maxMoves) {
            return;
        }

        // Run action
        this.makeNextAction();
    }
}
```

```java
/**
 * Map robot's sensor data to actions from binary string
 *
 * @param sensorActionsStr Binary GA chromosome
 * @return int[] An array to map sensor value to an action
 */
private int[] calcSensorActions(int[] sensorActionsStr){
    // How many actions are there?
    int numActions = (int) sensorActionsStr.length / 2;
    int sensorActions[] = new int[numActions];

    // Loop through actions
    for (int sensorValue = 0; sensorValue < numActions; sensorValue++){
        // Get sensor action
        int sensorAction = 0;
        if (sensorActionsStr[sensorValue*2] == 1){
            sensorAction += 2;
        }
        if (sensorActionsStr[(sensorValue*2)+1] == 1){
            sensorAction += 1;
        }

        // Add to sensor-action map
        sensorActions[sensorValue] = sensorAction;
    }

    return sensorActions;
}

/**
 * Runs the next action
 */
public void makeNextAction(){
    // If move forward
    if (this.getNextAction() == 1) {
        int currentX = this.xPosition;
        int currentY = this.yPosition;

        // Move depending on current direction
        if (Direction.NORTH == this.heading) {
            this.yPosition += -1;
            if (this.yPosition < 0) {
                this.yPosition = 0;
            }
        }
```

```
        else if (Direction.EAST == this.heading) {
            this.xPosition += 1;
            if (this.xPosition > this.maze.getMaxX()) {
                this.xPosition = this.maze.getMaxX();
            }
        }
        else if (Direction.SOUTH == this.heading) {
            this.yPosition += 1;
            if (this.yPosition > this.maze.getMaxY()) {
                this.yPosition = this.maze.getMaxY();
            }
        }
        else if (Direction.WEST == this.heading) {
            this.xPosition += -1;
            if (this.xPosition < 0) {
                this.xPosition = 0;
            }
        }

        // We can't move here
        if (this.maze.isWall(this.xPosition, this.yPosition) == true) {
            this.xPosition = currentX;
            this.yPosition = currentY;
        }
        else {
            if(currentX != this.xPosition || currentY
            != this.yPosition) {
                this.route.add(this.getPosition());
            }
        }
    }
    // Move clockwise
    else if(this.getNextAction() == 2) {
        if (Direction.NORTH == this.heading) {
            this.heading = Direction.EAST;
        }
        else if (Direction.EAST == this.heading) {
            this.heading = Direction.SOUTH;
        }
        else if (Direction.SOUTH == this.heading) {
            this.heading = Direction.WEST;
        }
        else if (Direction.WEST == this.heading) {
            this.heading = Direction.NORTH;
        }
    }
```

```
    // Move anti-clockwise
    else if(this.getNextAction() == 3) {
        if (Direction.NORTH == this.heading) {
            this.heading = Direction.WEST;
        }
        else if (Direction.EAST == this.heading) {
            this.heading = Direction.NORTH;
        }
        else if (Direction.SOUTH == this.heading) {
            this.heading = Direction.EAST;
        }
        else if (Direction.WEST == this.heading) {
            this.heading = Direction.SOUTH;
        }
    }

    // Reset sensor value
    this.sensorVal = -1;
}

/**
 * Get next action depending on sensor mapping
 *
 * @return int Next action
 */
public int getNextAction() {
    return this.sensorActions[this.getSensorValue()];
}

/**
 * Get sensor value
 *
 * @return int Next sensor value
 */
public int getSensorValue(){
    // If sensor value has already been calculated
    if (this.sensorVal > -1) {
        return this.sensorVal;
    }

        boolean frontSensor, frontLeftSensor, frontRightSensor,
        leftSensor, rightSensor, backSensor;
        frontSensor = frontLeftSensor = frontRightSensor =
        leftSensor = rightSensor = backSensor = false;
```

```
// Find which sensors have been activated
if (this.getHeading() == Direction.NORTH) {
    frontSensor = this.maze.isWall(this.xPosition,
    this.yPosition-1);
    frontLeftSensor = this.maze.isWall(this.xPosition-1,
    this.yPosition-1);
    frontRightSensor = this.maze.isWall(this.xPosition+1,
    this.yPosition-1);
    leftSensor = this.maze.isWall(this.xPosition-1,
    this.yPosition);
    rightSensor = this.maze.isWall(this.xPosition+1,
    this.yPosition);
    backSensor = this.maze.isWall(this.xPosition,
    this.yPosition+1);
}
else if (this.getHeading() == Direction.EAST) {
    frontSensor = this.maze.isWall(this.xPosition+1,
    this.yPosition);
    frontLeftSensor = this.maze.isWall(this.xPosition+1,
    this.yPosition-1);
    frontRightSensor = this.maze.isWall(this.xPosition+1,
    this.yPosition+1);
    leftSensor = this.maze.isWall(this.xPosition,
    this.yPosition-1);
    rightSensor = this.maze.isWall(this.xPosition,
    this.yPosition+1);
    backSensor = this.maze.isWall(this.xPosition-1,
    this.yPosition);
}
else if (this.getHeading() == Direction.SOUTH) {
    frontSensor = this.maze.isWall(this.xPosition,
    this.yPosition+1);
    frontLeftSensor = this.maze.isWall(this.xPosition+1,
    this.yPosition+1);
    frontRightSensor = this.maze.isWall(this.xPosition-1,
    this.yPosition+1);
    leftSensor = this.maze.isWall(this.xPosition+1,
    this.yPosition);
    rightSensor = this.maze.isWall(this.xPosition-1,
    this.yPosition);
    backSensor = this.maze.isWall(this.xPosition,
    this.yPosition-1);
}
else {
    frontSensor = this.maze.isWall(this.xPosition-1,
    this.yPosition);
    frontLeftSensor = this.maze.isWall(this.xPosition-1,
    this.yPosition+1);
```

```
            frontRightSensor = this.maze.isWall(this.xPosition-1,
            this.yPosition-1);
            leftSensor = this.maze.isWall(this.xPosition,
            this.yPosition+1);
            rightSensor = this.maze.isWall(this.xPosition,
            this.yPosition-1);
            backSensor = this.maze.isWall(this.xPosition+1,
            this.yPosition);
        }

        // Calculate sensor value
        int sensorVal = 0;

        if (frontSensor == true) {
            sensorVal += 1;
        }
        if (frontLeftSensor == true) {
            sensorVal += 2;
        }
        if (frontRightSensor == true) {
            sensorVal += 4;
        }
        if (leftSensor == true) {
            sensorVal += 8;
        }
        if (rightSensor == true) {
            sensorVal += 16;
        }
        if (backSensor == true) {
            sensorVal += 32;
        }

        this.sensorVal = sensorVal;

        return sensorVal;
    }
    /**
     * Get robot's position
     *
     * @return int[] Array with robot's position
     */
    public int[] getPosition(){
        return new int[]{this.xPosition, this.yPosition};
    }
```

```java
/**
 * Get robot's heading
 *
 * @return Direction Robot's heading
 */
private Direction getHeading(){
    return this.heading;
}

/**
 * Returns robot's complete route around the maze
 *
 * @return ArrayList<int> Robot's route
 */
public ArrayList<int[]> getRoute(){
    return this.route;
}

/**
 * Returns route in printable format
 *
 * @return String Robot's route
 */
public String printRoute(){
    String route = "";

    for (Object routeStep : this.route) {
        int step[] = (int[]) routeStep;
        route += "{" + step[0] + "," + step[1] + "}";
    }
    return route;
}
}
```

This class contains the constructor to create a new Robot. It also contains functions to read the robot's sensors, to get the robot's heading and to move the robot around the maze. This Robot class is our way of simulating a simple robot so that we don't have to run 1,000 generations of evolution on a population of 100 *actual* robots. You'll often find classes like Maze and Robot in optimization problems like these, where it's cost effective to simulate via software before refining your results in production hardware.

Recall that it's technically the Maze class that evaluates the fitness of a route. However, we still need to implement the calcFitness method in our GeneticAlgorithm class. Rather than calculating the fitness score directly, the calcFitness method is responsible for tying together the Individual, Robot, and Maze classes by creating a new Robot with the Individual's chromosome (i.e., sensor controller instruction set) and evaluating it against our Maze.

Write the following calcFitness function in the GeneticAlgorithm class. As always, this method can go anywhere in the class.

```
public double calcFitness(Individual individual, Maze maze) {
      int[] chromosome = individual.getChromosome();
      Robot robot = new Robot(chromosome, maze, 100);
      robot.run();
      int fitness = maze.scoreRoute(robot.getRoute());
      individual.setFitness(fitness);
      return fitness;
}
```

Here, the calcFitness method accepts two parameters, individual and maze, which it uses to create a new robot and run it through the maze. The robot's route is then scored and stored as the individual's fitness.

This code will create a robot, place it in our maze and test it using the evolved controller. The final parameter of the Robot constructor is the max number of moves the robot is allowed to make. This will prevent it from getting stuck in dead ends, or moving around in never ending circles. We can then simply take the score of the robot's route and return it as the fitness using Maze's scoreRoute method.

With a working calcFitness method, we can now create an evalPopulation method. Recall from Chapter 2 that the evalPopulation method simply loops over each individual in the population and calls calcFitness for that individual, summing the total population fitness as it goes. In fact, this chapter's evalPopulation is almost equivalent to Chapter 2's – but in this case, we also need to pass the maze object to the calcFitness method, so we need a slight modification.

Add the following method to the GeneticAlgorithm class, anywhere you like:

```
public void evalPopulation(Population population, Maze maze) {
      double populationFitness = 0;

      for (Individual individual : population.getIndividuals()) {
            populationFitness += this.calcFitness(individual, maze);
      }

      population.setPopulationFitness(populationFitness);
}
```

The only difference between this version and Chapter 2's version is the inclusion of "Maze maze" as the second parameter, and also the passing of "maze" as the second parameter to calcFitness.

At this point, you can resolve the two "TODO: Evaluate population" lines in the RobotController's "main" method. Find the two locations that show:

```
// TODO: Evaluate population
```

and replace them with:

```
// Evaluate population
ga.evalPopulation(population, maze);
```

Unlike Chapter 2, this method requires passing the maze object as the second parameter. At this point, you should only have five "TODO" comments left in RobotController's main method. We'll quickly take care of three more of them in the next section. That's progress!

Termination Check

The termination check we will use for this implementation is slightly different from the one used in our previous genetic algorithm. Here, we are going to terminate after a maximum number of generations have passed.

To add this termination check, begin by adding the following isTerminationConditionMet method to the GeneticAlgorithm class.

```
public boolean isTerminationConditionMet(int generationsCount, int
maxGenerations) {
        return (generationsCount > maxGenerations);
    }
```

This method simply accepts the current generation counter and the maximum generations allowed and returns true or false depending on if the algorithm should terminate or not. Truthfully, this is simple enough that we could use the logic directly in the genetic algorithm loop's "while" condition – however, in favor of consistency, we'll always implement the termination condition check as a method in the GeneticAlgorithm class, even if it's a trivial method like the one above.

Now we can apply our termination check to the evolution loop by adding the following code to RobotController's main method. We simply pass through the number of generations and the maximum number of generations as parameters.

By adding the termination condition to the "while" statement you're essentially making the loop functional, so we should also take this opportunity to print out some stats and debug information.

The changes below are straightforward: first, update the "while" conditional to use ga.isTerminationConditionMet. Second, add calls to population.getFittest and System.out.println both in the loop and after it in order to display progress and results.

Here's what the RobotController class should look like at this point; we've just eliminated three more TODOs and only have two left:

```
package chapter3;

public class RobotController {

    public static int maxGenerations = 1000;

    public static void main(String[] args) {

        Maze maze = new Maze(new int[][] {
            { 0, 0, 0, 0, 1, 0, 1, 3, 2 },
            { 1, 0, 1, 1, 1, 0, 1, 3, 1 },
            { 1, 0, 0, 1, 3, 3, 3, 3, 1 },
            { 3, 3, 3, 1, 3, 1, 1, 0, 1 },
            { 3, 1, 3, 3, 3, 1, 1, 0, 0 },
            { 3, 3, 1, 1, 1, 1, 0, 1, 1 },
            { 1, 3, 0, 1, 3, 3, 3, 3, 3 },
            { 0, 3, 1, 1, 3, 1, 0, 1, 3 },
            { 1, 3, 3, 3, 3, 1, 1, 1, 4 }
        });

        // Create genetic algorithm
        GeneticAlgorithm ga = new GeneticAlgorithm(200, 0.05,
        0.9, 2, 10);
        Population population = ga.initPopulation(128);

        // Evaluate population
        ga.evalPopulation(population, maze);

        int generation = 1;

        // Start evolution loop
        while (ga.isTerminationConditionMet(generation,
        maxGenerations) == false) {
            // Print fittest individual from population
            Individual fittest = population.getFittest(0);
            System.out.println("G" + generation + " Best solution
            (" + fittest.getFitness() + "): " + fittest.
            toString());

            // TODO: Apply crossover

            // TODO: Apply mutation
```

```
                    // Evaluate population
                    ga.evalPopulation(population, maze);

                    // Increment the current generation
                    generation++;
            }

            System.out.println("Stopped after " + maxGenerations + "
            generations.");
            Individual fittest = population.getFittest(0);
            System.out.println("Best solution
            (" + fittest.getFitness() + "): " + fittest.toString());

        }
}
```

If you were to hit the Run button now, you'd watch the algorithm quickly loop through 1,000 generations (with no actual evolution!) and proudly present to you a very, very bad solution with a fitness of, statistically speaking, most likely 1.0.

This is unsurprising; we still haven't implemented crossover or mutation! As you learned in Chapter 2, you need at least one of those mechanisms to drive evolution forward, but generally, you want both in order to avoid getting stuck in a local optimum.

We have two TODOs left in the main method above, and fortunately, we can resolve one of them very quickly. The mutation technique we learned in Chapter 2 – bit flip mutation – is also valid for this problem.

When evaluating the feasibility of a mutation or crossover algorithm, you must first consider the constraints on what's considered a valid chromosome. In this case, for this specific problem, a valid chromosome only has two constraints: it must be binary, and it must be 128 bits long. As long as those two constraints are met, there is no combination or sequence of bits that is considered invalid. So, we're able to reuse our simple mutation method from Chapter 2.

Enabling mutation is simple, and is the same as in last chapter. Update the "TODO: Mutate population" line to reflect the following:

```
// Apply mutation
population = ga.mutatePopulation(population);
```

Try running the program again at this point. The results aren't spectacular; you may get a fitness score of 5 or 10 after 1,000 generations. However, one thing is clear: the population is now evolving, and we're getting closer to the finish.

We have only one TODO remaining: crossover.

Selection Method and Crossover

In our previous genetic algorithm, we used roulette wheel selection to choose the parents for a uniform crossover operation. Recall that crossover is a category of techniques used to combine the genetic information of two parents. In this implementation, we are going to use a new selection method called *tournament selection and* a new crossover method called *single point crossover*.

Tournament Selection

Like roulette wheel selection, tournament selection provides a method for selecting individuals based on their fitness value. That is, the higher an individual's fitness the greater the chance that the individual will be chosen for crossover.

Tournament selection selects its parents by running a series of "tournaments". First, individuals are randomly selected from the population and entered into a tournament. Next, these individuals can be thought to compete with each other by comparing their fitness values, then choosing the individual with the highest fitness for the parent.

Tournament selection requires a tournament size to be defined that specifies how many individuals from the population it should pick to compete in a tournament. As with most parameters, there is a tradeoff in performance depending on the value chosen. A high tournament size will consider a larger proportion of the population. This makes it much more likely to find the higher scoring individuals in the population. Alternately, a low tournament size will select individuals from the population more randomly due to less competition, often picking lower ranking individuals as a result. A high tournament size can lead to a loss of genetic diversity where only the best individuals are being selected as parents. Conversely, a low tournament size can slow progress of the algorithm due to the reduced selection pressure.

Tournament selection is one of the most common selection methods used in genetic algorithms. Its strengths being that it's a relatively simple algorithm to implement and allows for variable selection pressure by updating the tournament size. It does have limitations however. Consider when the lowest scoring individual is placed into a tournament. It wouldn't matter what other individuals from the population are added to the tournament, it will never be chosen because the other individuals are guaranteed to have a higher fitness value. This drawback could be resolved by adding a selection probability to the algorithm. For example, if the selection probability is set to 0.6, there would be a 60% chance the fittest individual is selected. If the fittest individual isn't selected, it will then move on to the second fittest individual and so on until an individual has been picked. While this modification allows even the worst ranking individuals to be selected occasionally, it doesn't take into account the fitness difference between individuals. For example, if three individuals were chosen for tournament selection, one having a fitness value of 9, one with a fitness value of 2, and the other with a fitness value of 1. In this case, the individual with a fitness value of 2 would be no more likely to be picked if the fitness value was 8. This means occasionally individuals are given unreasonably high or low odds for selection.

We will not implement selection probability in our tournament selection implementation; however, it is an excellent exercise for the reader.

To implement tournament selection add the following code to the GeneticAlgorithm class, anywhere you like:

```java
public Individual selectParent(Population population) {
    // Create tournament
    Population tournament = new Population(this.tournamentSize);

    // Add random individuals to the tournament
    population.shuffle();
    for (int i = 0; i < this.tournamentSize; i++) {
        Individual tournamentIndividual = population.getIndividual(i);
        tournament.setIndividual(i, tournamentIndividual);
    }

    // Return the best
    return tournament.getFittest(0);
}
```

First, we create a new population to hold all the individuals in the selection tournament. Next, individuals are randomly added to the population until its size equals the tournament size parameter. Finally, the best individual from the tournament population is selected and returned.

Single Point Crossover

Single point crossover is an alternative crossover method to the uniform crossover method we implemented previously. Single point crossover is a very simple crossover method in which a single position in the genome is chosen at random to define which genes come from which parent. The genetic information before the crossover position comes from parent1, while the genetic information, after the position, comes from parent2.

Parent 1	1	0	0	1	1
Parent 2	0	0	1	1	0
Offspring	1	0	1	1	0

Single point crossover is reasonably easy to implement and allows contiguous groups of bits to be transferred from parents more effectively than in uniform crossover. This is a valuable property of crossover algorithms. Consider our specific problem, where the chromosome is an encoded set of instructions based on six sensor inputs, *and* each instruction is more than one bit long.

Imagine an ideal crossover situation as follows: parent1 is great at the first 32 sensor operations, and parent2 is great at, say, the last 16 operations. If we were to use the uniform crossover technique from Chapter 2, we'd get jumbled bits everywhere! Individual instructions would be changed and corrupted in the crossover due to the uniform crossover choosing bits at random to exchange. The two-bit instructions may not be preserved at all, because one of the two bits per each instruction might get modified. However, single point crossover lets us capitalize on this ideal situation. If the crossover point is directly in the middle of the chromosome, the offspring would end up with 64 uninterrupted bits representing 32 instructions from parent1, *and* the great 16 instructions from parent2 as well. So, the offspring now excels at 48 of the 64 possible states. This concept is the underpinning of genetic algorithms: that the offspring may be stronger than either parent because it takes the best qualities from both.

Single point crossover is not without its limitations, however. One limitation of single point crossover is that some combinations the parents' genomes are simply not possible. For example, consider two parents: one with a genome of "00100" and the other with a genome of "10001". The child "10101" isn't possible with crossover alone, although the genes required are available in the two parents. Fortunately, we also have mutation as an evolution mechanism, and the genome "10101" *is* possible if both crossover and mutation are implemented.

Another limitation of single point crossover is that genes toward the left have a bias of coming from parent1, and genes towards the right have a bias of coming from parent2. To address this problem, two-point crossover can be implemented where two positions are used allowing the partition to span the edges of the parent's genome. We leave two-point crossover as an exercise for the reader.

Parent 1	1	0	0	1	1
Parent 2	0	0	1	1	0
Offspring	1	0	1	1	1

End position   Start position

To implement single point crossover, add the following code to the GeneticAlgorithm class. This crossoverPopulation method relies on the selectParent method you implemented above, and therefore uses tournament selection. Note that there is no requirement to use tournament selection with single point crossover; you can use any implementation of selectParent, however for this problem we've chosen tournament selection and single point crossover since they're both very common and important concepts to understand.

```
public Population crossoverPopulation(Population population) {
      // Create new population
      Population newPopulation = new Population(population.size());

      // Loop over current population by fitness
      for (int populationIndex = 0; populationIndex <
      population.size(); populationIndex++) {
            Individual parent1 = population.getFittest(populationIndex);

            // Apply crossover to this individual?
            if (this.crossoverRate > Math.random() && populationIndex >=
            this.elitismCount) {
                  // Initialize offspring
                  Individual offspring = new Individual
                  (parent1.getChromosomeLength());

                  // Find second parent
                  Individual parent2 = this.selectParent(population);

                  // Get random swap point
                  int swapPoint = (int) (Math.random() *
                  (parent1.getChromosomeLength() + 1));
```

```
            // Loop over genome
            for (int geneIndex = 0; geneIndex < parent1.
            getChromosomeLength(); geneIndex++) {
                    // Use half of parent1's genes and half of
                    parent2's genes
                    if (geneIndex < swapPoint) {
                            offspring.setGene(geneIndex,
                            parent1.getGene(geneIndex));
                    } else {
                            offspring.setGene(geneIndex,
                            parent2.getGene(geneIndex));
                    }
            }

            // Add offspring to new population
            newPopulation.setIndividual(populationIndex,
            offspring);
        } else {
            // Add individual to new population without applying
            crossover
            newPopulation.setIndividual(populationIndex, parent1);
        }
    }

    return newPopulation;
}
```

Note that while we've made no mention of elitism in this chapter, it's still represented above and in the mutation algorithm (which was unchanged from the previous chapter).

Single point crossover is popular both because of its favorable genetic attributes (preserving contiguous genes), and because it's easy to implement. In the code above, a new population is created for the new individuals. Next, the population is looped over and individuals are fetched in order of fitness. If elitism is enabled, the elite individuals are skipped over and added straight into the new population, otherwise it's decided whether to crossover the current individual based on the crossover rate. If the individual is chosen for crossover, a second parent is picked using tournament selection.

Next, a crossover point is picked at random. This is the point at which we'll stop using parent1's genes and start using parent2's genes. Then we simply loop over the chromosome, adding parent1's genes to the offspring at first, and then switching to parent2's genes after the crossover point.

Now we can invoke crossover in the RobotController's main method. Adding the line "population = ga.crossoverPopulation(population)" resolves our final TODO, and you should be left with a RobotController class that looks like the following:

```java
package chapter3;

public class RobotController {

	public static int maxGenerations = 1000;

	public static void main(String[] args) {

		Maze maze = new Maze(new int[][] {
			{ 0, 0, 0, 0, 1, 0, 1, 3, 2 },
			{ 1, 0, 1, 1, 1, 0, 1, 3, 1 },
			{ 1, 0, 0, 1, 3, 3, 3, 3, 1 },
			{ 3, 3, 3, 1, 3, 1, 1, 0, 1 },
			{ 3, 1, 3, 3, 3, 1, 1, 0, 0 },
			{ 3, 3, 1, 1, 1, 1, 0, 1, 1 },
			{ 1, 3, 0, 1, 3, 3, 3, 3, 3 },
			{ 0, 3, 1, 1, 3, 1, 0, 1, 3 },
			{ 1, 3, 3, 3, 3, 1, 1, 1, 4 }
		});

		// Create genetic algorithm
		GeneticAlgorithm ga = new GeneticAlgorithm(200, 0.05,
		0.9, 2, 10);
		Population population = ga.initPopulation(128);

		// Evaluate population
		ga.evalPopulation(population, maze);

		int generation = 1;

		// Start evolution loop
		while (ga.isTerminationConditionMet(generation,
		maxGenerations) == false) {
			// Print fittest individual from population
			Individual fittest = population.getFittest(0);
			System.out.println("G" + generation + " Best solution
			(" + fittest.getFitness() + "): " + fittest.
			toString());

			// Apply crossover
			population = ga.crossoverPopulation(population);
```

```
                // Apply mutation
                population = ga.mutatePopulation(population);

                // Evaluate population
                ga.evalPopulation(population, maze);

                // Increment the current generation
                generation++;
            }
            System.out.println("Stopped after " + maxGenerations + "
            generations.");
            Individual fittest = population.getFittest(0);
            System.out.println("Best solution
            (" + fittest.getFitness() + "): " + fittest.toString());
        }
}
```

Execution

At this point, your GeneticAlgorithm class should have the following properties and method signatures:

```
package chapter3;

public class GeneticAlgorithm {

        private int populationSize;
        private double mutationRate;
        private double crossoverRate;
        private int elitismCount;
        protected int tournamentSize;

        public GeneticAlgorithm(int populationSize, double mutationRate,
        double crossoverRate, int elitismCount, int tournamentSize) { }
        public Population initPopulation(int chromosomeLength) { }
        public double calcFitness(Individual individual, Maze maze) { }
        public void evalPopulation(Population population, Maze maze) { }
        public boolean isTerminationConditionMet(int generationsCount,
        int maxGenerations) { }
        public Individual selectParent(Population population) { }
        public Population mutatePopulation(Population population) { }
        public Population crossoverPopulation(Population population) { }

}
```

If your method signatures don't match the above, or if you've accidentally missed a method, or if your IDE shows any errors, you should go back and resolve them now.

Otherwise, click Run.

You should see 1,000 generations of evolution, and hopefully your algorithm ended with a fitness score of 29, which is the maximum for this particular maze. (You can count the number of "Route" tiles – represented by "3" – in the maze definition to get this number.

Recall that the purpose of this algorithm wasn't to solve a maze, it was to program a robot's sensor controllers. Presumably, we could now take the winning chromosome at the end of this execution and program it into a physical robot and have a high level of confidence that the sensor controller will make the appropriate maneuvers to navigate not just this maze, but *any* maze without crashing into walls. There's no guarantee that this robot will find the most efficient route through the maze, because that's not what we trained it to do, but it will at the very least not crash.

While 64 sensor combinations may not seem too daunting to program by hand, consider the same problem but in three dimensions: an autonomous flying quadcopter drone may have 20 sensors rather than 6. In this case, you'd have to program for 2^{20} combinations of sensor inputs, approximately one million different instructions.

Summary

Genetic algorithms can be used to design sophisticated controllers, which may be difficult or time consuming for a human to do manually. The robot controller is evaluated by the fitness function, which will often simulate the robot and its environment to save time by not needing to physically test the robot.

By giving the robot a maze and a preferred route, a genetic algorithm can be applied to find a controller that can use the robot's sensors to successfully navigate the maze. This can be done by assigning each sensor an action in the individual's chromosome encoding. By making small random changes with crossover and mutation, guided by the selection process, better controllers are gradually found.

Tournament selection is one of the more popular selection methods used in genetic algorithms. It works by picking a pre-decided number of individuals from the population at random, then comparing the chosen individual's fitness values to find the best. The individual with the highest fitness value "wins" the tournament, and is then returned as the selected individual. Larger tournament sizes lead to high selection pressure, which needs to be carefully considered when picking an optimal tournament size.

When an individual has been selected, it will undergo crossover; one of the crossover methods that could be used is single point crossover. In this crossover method, a single point in the chromosome is picked at random, then any genetic information before that point comes from parent A, and any genetic information after that point comes from parent B. This leads to a reasonably random mix of parent's genetic information, however often the improved two-point crossover method is used instead. In two-point crossover, a start and end point are picked which are used instead to select the genetic information that comes from parent A and the remaining genetic information then comes from parent B.

Exercises

1. Add a second termination condition that terminates the algorithm when the route has been fully explored.

2. Run the algorithm with different tournament sizes. Study how the performance is affected.

3. Add a selection probability to the tournament selection method. Test with different probability settings. Examine how it affects the genetic algorithm's performance.

4. Implement two-point crossover. Does it improve the results?

Traveling Salesman

Chapter 4

Introduction

In this chapter, we are going to explore the traveling salesman problem and how it can be solved using a genetic algorithm. In doing so, we will be looking at the properties of the traveling salesman problem and how we can use those properties to design the genetic algorithm.

The traveling salesman problem (TSP) is a classic optimization problem, studied as far back as the 1800s. The traveling salesman problem involves finding the most efficient route through a collection of cities, visiting each city exactly once.

The traveling salesman problem is often described in terms of optimizing a route through a collection of cities; however, the traveling salesman problem can be applied to other applications. For example, the notion of cities can be thought of as customers for certain applications, or even as soldering points on a microchip. The idea of distance can also be revised to consider other constraints such as time.

In its simplest form, cities can be represented as nodes on a graph, with the distance between each city represented by the length of the edges (see Figure 4-1). A "route" or a "tour", simply defines which edges should be used, and in what order. The route's score can then be calculated by summing the edges used in the route.

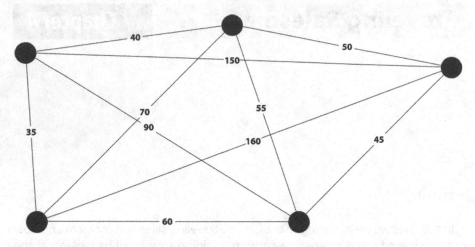

Figure 4-1. Our graph showing the cities and the respective distances between them

During the 1900s, the traveling salesman problem was studied by many mathematicians and scientists; however to this day the problem remains unsolved. The only guaranteed method to produce an optimal solution for the traveling salesman problem is by using a brute force algorithm. A brute force algorithm is an algorithm designed to systematically try every possible solution. Then you find the optimal solution from the complete set of candidate solutions. Attempting solving the traveling salesman problem with a brute force algorithm is an extremely hard task because the number of potential solutions experiences factorial growth as the number of cities is increased. Factorial functions grow even faster than exponential functions, which is why it's so hard to brute force the traveling salesman problem. For example, for 5 cities, there are 120 possible solutions (1x2x3x4x5), and for 10 cities that number will have increased to 3,628,800 solutions! By 15 cities, there are over a trillion solutions. At 60 cities, there are more possible solutions than there are atoms in the observable universe.

Brute force algorithms can be used to find optimal solutions when there are only a few cities but they become more and more challenging as the number of cities increase. Even when techniques are applied to remove reverse and identical routes, it still becomes quickly infeasible to find an optimal solution in a reasonable amount of time.

In reality, we know that finding an optimal solution usually isn't necessary because a good enough solution will typically be all that's required. There are a number of different algorithms that can quickly find solutions that are likely to be within only a couple of percent of optimal. One of the more commonly used algorithms is the nearest neighbor algorithm. With this algorithm, a starting city is picked at random. Then, the next nearest unvisited city is found and picked as the second city in the route. This process of picking the next nearest the unvisited city is continued until all cities have been visited and a complete route has been found. The nearest neighbor algorithm has been shown to be surprisingly effective at producing reasonable solutions that score within a fraction the optimal solution. Better still, this can be done in a very short time frame. These characteristics make it an attractive solution in many situations, and a possible alternative to genetic algorithms.

The Problem

The problem we will be tackling in this implementation is a typical traveling salesman problem in which we need to optimize a route through a collection of cities. We can generate a number of random cities in 2D space by setting each city to a random x, y position.

When finding the distance between two cities we will simply use the shortest length between the cities as the distance. We can calculate this distance with the following equation:

$$Distance = \sqrt{\left(x_a - x_b\right)^2 + \left(y_a - y_b\right)^2}$$

Often, the problem will be more complex than this. In this example we are assuming a direct ideal path exists between each city; this is also known as the "Euclidean distance". This usually isn't going to be a typical case as there could be various obstacles making the actual shortest path much longer than the Euclidean distance. We are also assuming that traveling from City-A to City-B takes just as long as traveling from City-B to City-A. Again, in reality this is rarely the case. Often there will be obstacles such as one-way roads that will affect the distance between cities while traveling in a certain direction. An implementation of the traveling salesman problem where the distance between the cities changes depending on the direction is called an *asymmetric traveling salesman problem*.

Implementation

It is time to go ahead and tackle the problem using our knowledge of genetic algorithms. After setting up a new Java/Eclipse package for this problem, we'll begin by encode the route.

Before You Start

This chapter will build on the code you developed in Chapter 3. Before you start, create a new Eclipse or NetBeans project, or create a new package in your existing project for this book called "chapter4".

Copy the Individual, Population, and GeneticAlgorithm classes over from Chapter 3 and import them into chapter4. Make sure to update the package name at the top of each class file! They should all say "package chapter4" at the very top.

Open the GeneticAlgorithm class and delete the following methods: calcFitness, evalPopulation, crossoverPopulation, and mutatePopulation. You'll rewrite those methods in the course of this chapter.

Next, open the Individual class and delete the constructor with the signature "public Individual(int chromosomeLength)". There are two constructors in the Individual class, so be careful to delete the correct one! The constructor to delete is the one that randomly initializes the chromosome; you'll rewrite that as well in this chapter.

The Population class from Chapter 3 requires no modifications other than the package name at the top of the file.

Encoding

The encoding we choose in this example will need to be able to encode a list of cities *in order*. We can do this by assigning each city a unique ID then referencing it using a chromosome in the order of the candidate route. This type of encoding where sequences of genes are used is known as *permutation encoding* and is very well suited to the traveling salesman problem.

The first thing we need to do is assign our cities unique IDs. If we have 5 cities to visit, we can simply assign them the IDs: 1,2,3,4,5. Then when our genetic algorithm has found a route, our chromosome may order the city IDs to look like the following: 3,4,1,2,5. This simply means we would start at city 3, then travel to city 4, then city 1, then city 2, then city 5, before returning back to city 3 to complete the route.

Initialization

Before we start optimizing a route, we need to create some cities. As mentioned earlier, we can generate random cities by picking random x,y coordinates and using them to define a city location.

First, we need to create a City class, which can create and store a city as well as calculate the shortest distance to another city.

```
package chapter4;
public class City {
        private int x;
        private int y;
```

```
    public City(int x, int y) {
        this.x = x;
        this.y = y;
    }

    public double distanceFrom(City city) {
        // Give difference in x,y
        double deltaXSq = Math.pow((city.getX() - this.getX()), 2);
        double deltaYSq = Math.pow((city.getY() - this.getY()), 2);

        // Calculate shortest path
        double distance = Math.sqrt(Math.abs(deltaXSq + deltaYSq));
        return distance;
    }

    public int getX() {
        return this.x;
    }

    public int getY() {
        return this.y;
    }
}
```

The City class has a constructor that takes an x and y coordinate to create a city on a 2D plane. The class also contains a distanceFrom method that calculates the straight-line distance from the current city to another city using the Pythagorean Theorem. Finally, there are two getter methods which can be used to retrieve the city's x and y position.

Next, we should reinstate the Individual class constructor we deleted in the "Before You Start" section. The traveling salesman problem has different constraints on the chromosome from those of our last two problems. Recall that the only constraints in the robot controller problem were that the chromosome must be 128 bits long, and that it must be binary.

Unfortunately, this is not the case with the traveling salesman problem; the constraints are more involved and dictate the initialization, crossover, and mutation techniques we can use. In this case, the chromosome must be of a certain length (however long the city tour is), but an additional constraint is that each city must be visited once and only once, otherwise the chromosome is invalid. There can be no duplicate genes in the chromosome, and there can be no omitted cities in the chromosome.

We can easily create a naïve Individual constructor without any randomness. Simply create a chromosome with each city's index in it: 1, 2, 3, 4, 5, 6..., etc. Randomizing the initial chromosome is an exercise for the reader at the end of the chapter.

Add the following constructor to the Individual class. You can place this anywhere you like, but near the top is a good location for constructors. As always, comments and docblocks have been omitted here, but please see the provided Eclipse project accompanying this book for additional commentary.

```
public Individual(int chromosomeLength) {
        // Create random individual
        int[] individual;
        individual = new int[chromosomeLength];

        for (int gene = 0; gene < chromosomeLength; gene++) {
                individual[gene] = gene;
        }

        this.chromosome = individual;
}
```

At this point, we can create our executive class and its "main" method. Create a new Java class called "TSP" in package "chapter4" by using the File ➤ New ➤ Class menu item. As in Chapter 3, we'll stub out the genetic algorithm pseudocode with a number of TODOs so we can mark our progress through the implementation.

Let's also take this opportunity to initialize an array of 100 randomly generated City objects at the top of the "main" method. Simply generate random x and y coordinates and pass them to the City constructor. Make sure your TSP class looks like the following:

```
package chapter4;
public class TSP {
        public static int maxGenerations = 3000;
        public static void main(String[] args) {

                int numCities = 100;
                City cities[] = new City[numCities];

                // Loop to create random cities
                for (int cityIndex = 0; cityIndex < numCities; cityIndex++) {
                        int xPos = (int) (100 * Math.random());
                        int yPos = (int) (100 * Math.random());
                        cities[cityIndex] = new City(xPos, yPos);
                }

                // Initial GA
                GeneticAlgorithm ga = new GeneticAlgorithm(100, 0.001, 0.9, 2, 5);
```

```
        // Initialize population
        Population population = ga.initPopulation(cities.length);

        // TODO: Evaluate population

        // Keep track of current generation
        int generation = 1;

        // Start evolution loop
        while (ga.isTerminationConditionMet(generation,
        maxGenerations) == false) {
                // TODO: Print fittest individual from population

                // TODO: Apply crossover

                // TODO: Apply mutation

                // TODO: Evaluate population

                // Increment the current generation
                generation++;
        }

        // TODO: Display results
    }
}
```

Hopefully, this procedure is becoming familiar; we're once again beginning to implement the pseudocode presented at the beginning of Chapter 2. We've also generated an array of City objects that we'll use in our evaluation methods, much like how we generated a Maze object to evaluate individuals against in the last chapter.

The rest is rote: initialize a GeneticAlgorithm object (including population size, mutation rate, crossover rate, elitism count, and tournament size), then initialize a population. The individuals' chromosome length must be the same as the number of cities we wish to visit.

We get to reuse the simple "max generations" termination condition from the previous chapter, so we're left with only six TODOs and a working loop this time. Let's begin, as usual, with the evaluation and fitness scoring methods.

Evaluation

Now we need to evaluate the population and assign fitness values to the individuals so we know which perform the best. The first step is to define the fitness function for the problem. Here, we simply need to calculate the total distance of the route given by the individual's chromosome.

First, we need to create a new class that can store a route and calculate its total distance. Create a new class called "Route" in package "chapter4" and insert the following code:

```java
package chapter4;

public class Route {
        private City route[];
        private double distance = 0;

        public Route(Individual individual, City cities[]) {
                // Get individual's chromosome
                int chromosome[] = individual.getChromosome();
                // Create route
                this.route = new City[cities.length];
                for (int geneIndex = 0; geneIndex < chromosome.length;
                geneIndex++) {
                        this.route[geneIndex] = cities[chromosome[geneIndex]];
                }
        }

        public double getDistance() {
                if (this.distance > 0) {
                        return this.distance;
                }

                // Loop over cities in route and calculate route distance
                double totalDistance = 0;
                for (int cityIndex = 0; cityIndex + 1 < this.route.length;
                cityIndex++) {
                        totalDistance += this.route[cityIndex].
                        distanceFrom(this.route[cityIndex + 1]);
                }

                totalDistance += this.route[this.route.length - 1]
                .distanceFrom(this.route[0]);
                this.distance = totalDistance;

                return totalDistance;
        }
}
```

This class contains only a constructor and a single method to calculate the total route distance. The constructor accepts an Individual and a list of City definitions (the same City array we created in the TSP class' "main" function). The constructor then builds an array of City objects in the order of the Individual's chromosome; this data structure makes it simple to evaluate the total route distance in the getDistance method.

The getDistance method loops through the route array (an ordered array of City objects) and calls the City class' "distanceFrom" method to calculate the distance between each two cities in turn, summing as it goes.

To implement this fitness scoring method, we need to update the calcFitness function in the GeneticAlgorithm class. The calcFitness class should delegate the distance calculation to the Route class and, in order to do so, it needs to accept our City definition array and pass it to the Route class.

Add the following method to the GeneticAlgorithm class, anywhere in the file.

```
public double calcFitness(Individual individual, City cities[]){
    // Get fitness
    Route route = new Route(individual, cities);
    double fitness = 1 / route.getDistance();

    // Store fitness
    individual.setFitness(fitness);
    return fitness;
}
```

In this function, the fitness is calculated by dividing 1 by the total route distance – a shorter distance therefore has a higher score. After the fitness has been calculated, it is stored for quick recall in case it is needed again.

Now we can update our evalPopulation method in the GeneticAlgorithm class to accept the cities parameter and find the fitness for every individual in the population.

```
public void evalPopulation(Population population, City cities[]){
    double populationFitness = 0;

    // Loop over population evaluating individuals and summing population
    fitness
    for (Individual individual : population.getIndividuals()) {
        populationFitness += this.calcFitness(individual, cities);
    }

    double avgFitness = populationFitness / population.size();
    population.setPopulationFitness(avgFitness);
}
```

As usual, this function loops over the population and each individual's fitness is calculated. Unlike previous implementations, we're calculating an average population fitness instead of a total population fitness. (Since we're using tournament selection rather than roulette wheel selection, we don't actually need the population's fitness; nothing would change if we simply didn't record this value.)

At this point, we can now resolve four of our TODOs in the TSP class' "main" method related to evaluation and displaying results. Update the TSP class to represent the following. The four TODOs resolved were the two "Evaluate population" lines (before the loop and inside the loop), the "Print fittest individual from population" line at the top of the loop, and the "Display results" line after the loop.

```java
package chapter4;
public class TSP {
        public static int maxGenerations = 3000;
        public static void main(String[] args) {
                int numCities = 100;
                City cities[] = new City[numCities];
                // Loop to create random cities
                for (int cityIndex = 0; cityIndex < numCities; cityIndex++) {
                        int xPos = (int) (100 * Math.random());
                        int yPos = (int) (100 * Math.random());
                        cities[cityIndex] = new City(xPos, yPos);
                }

                // Initial GA
                GeneticAlgorithm ga = new GeneticAlgorithm(100, 0.001,
                0.9, 2, 5);

                // Initialize population
                Population population = ga.initPopulation(cities.length);

                // Evaluate population
                ga.evalPopulation(population, cities);

                // Keep track of current generation
                int generation = 1;

                // Start evolution loop
                while (ga.isTerminationConditionMet(generation,
                maxGenerations) == false) {
                        // Print fittest individual from population
                        Route route = new Route(population.getFittest(0),
                        cities);
                        System.out.println("G"+generation+" Best distance: " +
                        route.getDistance());

                        // TODO: Apply crossover

                        // TODO: Apply mutation

                        // Evaluate population
                        ga.evalPopulation(population, cities);
```

```
            // Increment the current generation
            generation++;
        }

        // Display results
        System.out.println("Stopped after " + maxGenerations + "
        generations.");
        Route route = new Route(population.getFittest(0), cities);
        System.out.println("Best distance: " + route.getDistance());
    }
}
```

At this point, we can click "Run" and the loop will go through the motions, printing the same thing 3,000 times but showing no change. This, of course, is expected; we need to implement crossover and mutation as our two remaining TODOs.

Termination Check

As we have already learned, there is no way to know if we have found an optimal solution to the traveling salesman problem unless we try every possible solution. This means the termination check we use in this implementation cannot terminate when the optimal solution has been found, because it simply has no way of knowing.

Seeing as we have no way to terminate when the optimal solution has been found, we can simply allow the algorithm to run for a set number of generations before finally terminating, and therefore we are able to reuse the isTerminationConditionMet method in the GeneticAlgorithm class from Chapter 3.

Note, however, that in situations like these—where the best solution can not be known—that there are many sophisticated techniques for termination beyond simply setting an upper bound on the number of generations.

One common technique is to measure the improvement of the population's fitness over time. If the population is still improving rapidly, you may want to allow the algorithm to continue on. Once the population stops improving, you can end the evolution and present the best solution.

You may never find the globally optimum solution in a complex solution space like the traveling salesman problem's, but there are many strong local optima, and a plateau in progress typically indicates that you've found one of these local optima.

There are several ways you can measure the progress of a genetic algorithm over time. The simplest method is to measure the number of consecutive generations where there has been no improvement in the best individual. If the number of generations with no improvement has crossed some threshold, for instance 500 generations with no improvement, you can stop the algorithm.

One drawback of this simple approach with large solution spaces is that you may see constant improvement in the population's fitness – it just may be painfully slow! There are so many combinations that it's feasible to get a one-point improvement every dozen generations or so, and you'll never actually encounter 500 consecutive generations with no improvement. You could, of course, set a maximum upper bound on generations irrespective of improvement. You could also implement a more sophisticated technique, such as taking the moving average of various windows and comparing them against each other. If the fitness improvement has been trending downwards for several windows, stop the algorithm.

In our case, however, we'll stick with the naïve approach from Chapter 3, and leave it up to the reader to implement a better termination condition as an exercise at the end of the chapter.

Crossover

With the traveling salesman problem, both the genes and the order of the genes in the chromosome are very important. In fact, for the traveling salesman problem we shouldn't ever have more than one copy of a specific gene in our chromosome. This is because it would create an invalid solution because a city shouldn't be visited more than once on a given route. Consider a case where we have three cities: City A, City B and City C. A route of A,B,C is valid; however, a route of C,B,C is not: this route visits City C twice, and also never visits City A. Because of this, it's essential that we find and apply a crossover method that produces valid results for our problem.

We also need to be respectful of the ordering of the parent's chromosomes during the crossover process. This is because the order of the chromosome affects the solution's fitness. In fact, it's *only* the order that matters. To understand better why this is the case, consider how these following two routes are completely different even though they contain the exact same genes:

Route 1: A,B,C,D,E
Route 2: C,A,D,B,E

We previously looked at *uniform crossover*; however, the uniform crossover method works on the level of individual genes and doesn't respect the order of the chromosome. Single-point and two-point crossover methods do a better job as they deal with chunks of the chromosome, which will preserve order within those chunks. The problem with single-point and two-point crossover though, is that they aren't careful about which genes are being added and removed from the chromosome. This means we are likely to end up with invalid solutions with chromosomes that contain more than one reference for the same city or have cities missing altogether.

A crossover method, which addresses both these problems, is *ordered crossover*. In this crossover method, a subset of the first parent's chromosome is selected. That subset is then added to the child chromosome in the same position.

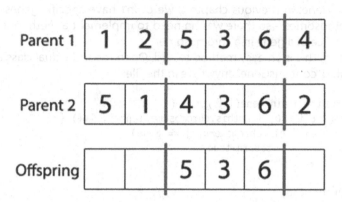

The next step is to add the second parent's genetic information to the offspring's chromosome. We do this by starting from the end position of the selected subset, and then include each gene from parent 2, which isn't already in the offspring's chromosome.

In this example, we would start from the gene "2" checking if it can be found in the offspring's chromosome. Because 2 isn't currently in the offspring's chromosome, we can add it to the first available position in the offspring's chromosome. Then, because we reached the end of parent 2's chromosome, we go back to the first gene, "5". This time the 5 is in the offspring's chromosome so we skip it and move onto the 1. We keep doing this until we end up with the following:

Parent 1	1	2	5	3	6	4
Parent 2	5	1	4	3	6	2
Offspring	2	1	5	3	6	4

This method of crossover retains a lot of the order from the parents, but also ensures solutions remain valid for problems such as the traveling salesman problem.

There's one aspect of this algorithm we can't pull off with our current Individual class: this technique requires checking the offspring's chromosome for the existence of a specific gene. In previous chapters, we didn't have specific genes – we had binary chromosomes – so there was no need to implement a method that checks for the existence of a gene in a chromosome.

Fortunately, this is an easy method to add. Open the Individual class and add a method called "containsGene" anywhere in the file:

```
public boolean containsGene(int gene) {
        for (int i = 0; i < this.chromosome.length; i++) {
                if (this.chromosome[i] == gene) {
                        return true;
                }
        }
        return false;
}
```

This method looks at each gene in the chromosome, and if it finds the gene it's looking for it will return true; otherwise it returns false. The usage of this method addresses the question: "Does this solution visit City #5? Let's call individual. containsGene(5) to find out."

We're now ready to apply our ordered crossover method to our genetic algorithm by updating the GeneticAlgorithm class. Like in the previous chapter, we can implement tournament selection as our selection method used for crossover, but we haven't modified the selectParent method from the last chapter.

Add this crossoverPopulation method to the GeneticAlgorithm class:

```
public Population crossoverPopulation(Population population){
    // Create new population
    Population newPopulation = new Population(population.size());

    // Loop over current population by fitness
    for (int populationIndex = 0; populationIndex < population.size();
    populationIndex++) {
        // Get parent1
        Individual parent1 = population.getFittest(populationIndex);

        // Apply crossover to this individual?
        if (this.crossoverRate > Math.random() && populationIndex >=
        this.elitismCount) {
            // Find parent2 with tournament selection
            Individual parent2 = this.selectParent(population);
```

```
// Create blank offspring chromosome
    int offspringChromosome[] = new
    int[parent1.getChromosomeLength()];
    Arrays.fill(offspringChromosome, -1);
    Individual offspring = new Individual(offspringChromosome);

    // Get subset of parent chromosomes
    int substrPos1 = (int) (Math.random() *
    parent1.getChromosomeLength());
    int substrPos2 = (int) (Math.random() *
    parent1.getChromosomeLength());

    // make the smaller the start and the larger the end
    final int startSubstr = Math.min(substrPos1, substrPos2);
    final int endSubstr = Math.max(substrPos1, substrPos2);

    // Loop and add the sub tour from parent1 to our child
    for (int i = startSubstr; i < endSubstr; i++) {
        offspring.setGene(i, parent1.getGene(i));
    }

    // Loop through parent2's city tour
    for (int i = 0; i < parent2.getChromosomeLength(); i++) {
        int parent2Gene = i + endSubstr;
        if (parent2Gene >= parent2.getChromosomeLength()) {
            parent2Gene -= parent2.getChromosomeLength();
        }

        // If offspring doesn't have the city add it
        if (offspring.containsGene
        (parent2.getGene(parent2Gene)) == false) {
            // Loop to find a spare position in the
            child's tour
            for (int ii = 0; ii <
            offspring.getChromosomeLength(); ii++) {
                // Spare position found, add city
                if (offspring.getGene(ii) == -1) {
                    offspring.setGene(ii,
                    parent2.getGene(parent2Gene));
                    break;
                }
            }
        }
    }
}
```

```
        // Add child
        newPopulation.setIndividual(populationIndex, offspring);
    } else {
        // Add individual to new population without applying
        crossover
        newPopulation.setIndividual(populationIndex, parent1);
    }
}

    return newPopulation;
}
```

In this method, we first create a new population to hold the offspring. Then, the current population is looped over in the order of the fittest individual first. If elitism is enabled, the first few elite individuals are skipped over and added to the new population unaltered. The remaining individuals are then considered for crossover using the crossover rate. If crossover is to be applied to the individual, a parent is selected using the selectParent method (in this case, selectParent implements tournament selection as in Chapter 3) and a new blank individual is created.

Next, two random positions in the parent1's chromosome are picked and the subset of genetic information between those positions are added to the offspring's chromosome. Finally, the remaining genetic information needed is added in the order found in parent2; then when complete, the individual is added into the new population.

We can now implement our crossoverPopulation method into our "main" method in the TSP class and resolve one of our TODOs. Find "TODO: Apply crossover" and replace it with:

```
// Apply crossover
population = ga.crossoverPopulation(population);
```

Clicking "Run" at this point should result in a working algorithm! After 3,000 generations, you should expect to see a best distance of approximately 1,500. However, as you may recall, crossover alone is prone to getting stuck in local optima, and you may find that the algorithm plateaus. Mutation is our way of randomly dropping candidates in new locations on our solution space, and can help improve long-term results at the cost of short-term gain.

Mutation

Like with crossover, the type of mutation we use for the traveling salesman problem is important because again, we need to ensure the chromosome is valid after it has been applied. A method in which we randomly change a single value of a gene would likely cause repeats in the chromosome and as a result, the chromosome would be invalid.

An easy solution to this is called *swap mutation*, which is an algorithm that will simply swap the genetic information at two points. Swap mutation works by looping though the genes in the individual's chromosome with each gene being considered for mutation determined by the mutation rate. If a gene is selected for mutation, another random gene in the chromosome is picked and then their positions are swapped.

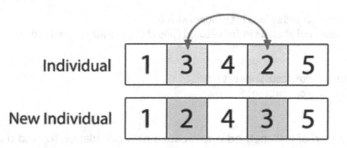

This process ensures no duplicate genes are created and that any resulting offspring will be valid solutions.

To implement this mutation method, first add the mutatePopulation method to the GeneticAlgorithm class.

```
public Population mutatePopulation(Population population){
    // Initialize new population
    Population newPopulation = new Population(this.populationSize);

    // Loop over current population by fitness
    for (int populationIndex = 0; populationIndex <
    population.size(); populationIndex++) {
        Individual individual =
        population.getFittest(populationIndex);

        // Skip mutation if this is an elite individual
        if (populationIndex >= this.elitismCount) {
            // System.out.println("Mutating population member
            "+populationIndex);
            // Loop over individual's genes
            for (int geneIndex = 0; geneIndex <
             individual.getChromosomeLength(); geneIndex++) {
            // Does this gene need mutation?
                if (this.mutationRate > Math.random()) {
                    // Get new gene position
                    int newGenePos = (int) (Math.random() *
                    individual.getChromosomeLength());
                    // Get genes to swap
                    int gene1 = individual.getGene(newGenePos);
```

```
                        int gene2 = individual.getGene(geneIndex);
                        // Swap genes
                        individual.setGene(geneIndex, gene1);
                        individual.setGene(newGenePos, gene2);
                }
            }
        }

        // Add individual to population
        newPopulation.setIndividual(populationIndex, individual);
    }

    // Return mutated population
    return newPopulation;
}
```

The first step of this method is to create a new population to hold the mutated individuals. Next, the population is looped over starting with the fittest individuals. If elitism is enabled, the first few individuals are skipped and added to the new population unaltered. The chromosomes from the remaining individuals are then looped over and each gene is considered for mutation individually depending on the mutation rate. If a gene is to be mutated, another random gene from the individual is picked and the genes are swapped. Finally, the mutated individual is added to the new population.

Now we can add the mutation method to our TSP class' "main" method and resolve our final TODO. Find the comment that says "TODO: Apply mutation" and replace it with:

```
// Apply mutation
population = ga.mutatePopulation(population);
```

Execution

The final code for the TSP class should look like this:

```
package chapter4;
public class TSP {
        public static int maxGenerations = 3000;
        public static void main(String[] args) {

                // Create cities
                int numCities = 100;
                City cities[] = new City[numCities];
```

```java
// Loop to create random cities
for (int cityIndex = 0; cityIndex < numCities; cityIndex++) {
    // Generate x,y position
    int xPos = (int) (100 * Math.random());
    int yPos = (int) (100 * Math.random());

    // Add city
    cities[cityIndex] = new City(xPos, yPos);
}

// Initial GA
GeneticAlgorithm ga = new GeneticAlgorithm(100, 0.001,
0.9, 2, 5);

// Initialize population
Population population = ga.initPopulation(cities.length);

// Evaluate population
//ga.evalPopulation(population, cities);

Route startRoute = new Route(population.getFittest(0), cities);
System.out.println("Start Distance: " + startRoute.getDistance());

// Keep track of current generation
int generation = 1;
// Start evolution loop
while (ga.isTerminationConditionMet(generation,
maxGenerations) == false) {
    // Print fittest individual from population
    Route route = new Route(population.getFittest(0),
    cities);
    System.out.println("G"+generation+" Best distance:
    " + route.getDistance());

    // Apply crossover
    population = ga.crossoverPopulation(population);

    // Apply mutation
    population = ga.mutatePopulation(population);

    // Evaluate population
    ga.evalPopulation(population, cities);

    // Increment the current generation
    generation++;
}
```

```
            System.out.println("Stopped after " + maxGenerations + "
            generations.");
            Route route = new Route(population.getFittest(0), cities);
            System.out.println("Best distance: " + route.getDistance());


      }
}
```

Additionally, check your GeneticAlgorithm class against the following properties and method signatures. If you missed implementing one of these methods, or one of your method signatures doesn't match, please go back and resolve the issue now.

```
package chapter4;
import java.util.Arrays;

public class GeneticAlgorithm {

      private int populationSize;
      private double mutationRate;
      private double crossoverRate;
      private int elitismCount;
      protected int tournamentSize;

      public GeneticAlgorithm(int populationSize, double mutationRate,
      double crossoverRate, int elitismCount, int tournamentSize) { }
      public Population initPopulation(int chromosomeLength){ }
      public boolean isTerminationConditionMet(int generationsCount,
      int maxGenerations) { }
      public double calcFitness(Individual individual, City cities[]) { }
      public void evalPopulation(Population population, City cities[]) { }
      public Individual selectParent(Population population) { }
      public Population crossoverPopulation(Population population) { }
      public Population mutatePopulation(Population population) { }

}
```

Finally, make sure you've updated the Individual class by replacing the constructor and adding the containsGene method.

At this point, click "Run" and observe the output. As usual, remind yourself that genetic algorithms are stochastic processes dictated by statistics, and that you can't make any conclusions based on just one trial. Unfortunately, the fact that this problem initializes a random set of cities means that each run of the program will have a different optimal solution; this makes experimenting with the genetic algorithm parameters and judging their performance difficult. The first exercise at the end of the chapter is to hard-code a list of cities so that you can accurately benchmark the algorithm's performance.

However, there are a few interesting observations you can make at this point. Run the algorithm a number of times and observe the best distance. Are they all similar? At least in the same ballpark? This is interesting, because each run uses a different set of cities. But upon reflection, it makes sense: while the cities are in different locations each time, there are still 100 of them every time, and they're still placed randomly on a 100x100 map, which means that we can estimate pretty easily the problem solution's total distance.

Consider a 100x100 map – which has an area of 10,000 units – but instead of visiting 100 cities, your goal is to visit 10,000 cities. If the cities are placed evenly on the map (one on each grid point), the best solution should be a distance of exactly 10,100 (visiting every tile on the map in a zigzag). If, instead of evenly distributing the cities, you were to randomly distribute those 10,000 cities, the best solution would be a statistical distribution centering at 10,000, varying slightly from run to run due to the randomness of the placement.

Now we can work backward and consider fewer cities; place only 25 cities evenly on the map and the shortest route is 600 units. The relationship here becomes clear: the distance is related to the square root of the map's area times the square root of the number of cities. Using this relationship we find that 100 cities placed evenly has a minimum distance of 1,100 (that's $\sqrt{(map)} * \sqrt{(numCities)} + \sqrt{(map)}$; the added square root term at the end accounts for the north-south travel, but we can drop that term when we start speaking statistically). If we place those same 100 cities randomly on our map, we can expect the minimum distance to be a distribution centering around 1,000. Similarly, 1,000 cities should have a best distance near 3,100.

If you play with the number of cities, you'll find that the algorithm easily confirms these suspicions for smaller numbers, but naturally, it has difficulty finding the minimum for more than 100 cities.

Now that we understand the relationship between the map size, the number of cities, and the expected best distance, we can experiment even without a constant set of cities and use our statistical expectations instead. One area of particular interest is the effect of mutation on the result quality.

If you imagine the solution space as a landscape of lots of rolling hills, a genetic algorithm is like dropping 100 people with different behaviors at random locations on the landscape and seeing which individual finds the lowest valley. (In this case, because our Individual constructor isn't random, we're actually dropping all individuals on the same spot.) Through the generations, individuals and their offspring will move downhill and then stop when they've found the lowest valley near them. Mutation, however, picks them up and drops them into a new random location – the location may be better or worse than the previous one, but at least it's a new, unique location that allows them to continue their search in a fresh landscape.

Mutation, however, can often have short-term detriments. Mutations can be either favorable or unfavorable – which is why we use elitism to protect the best individuals from mutation. However, the diversity that mutation introduces can have profound long-term effects, by placing an individual on a landscape that may otherwise not be explored: imagine a tall volcano with a huge chasm in the middle that contains the lowest point in the landscape (the global optimum, surrounded by unfavorable landscape). It's unlikely that any population would climb the volcano and find the global optimum at the center – unless a random mutation placed an individual on the lip of the volcano.

With that being said, observe the effects of different mutation rates and elitism counts on long-running (tens of thousands of generations) difficult problems (200 cities or more). Does mutation help or hurt? Does elitism help or hurt?

Summary

The traveling salesman problem is a classic optimization problem that asks: what is the shortest possible route between a list of cities, visiting each city once, and returning back to the initial city?

It is an unsolved optimization problem in which an optimal solution can only be found if a brute force algorithm is used. However, because the number of possible solutions to the traveling salesman problem grows so rapidly with each city added, it soon becomes infeasible to brute force solutions even with the most powerful computers. For these cases, heuristic methods are used to find a good approximation instead.

We covered a basic implementation of the traveling salesman problem using cities on a 2D graph and connected them by straight-line distance.

Using an ordered list of city IDs for the chromosomes' encoding, we were able to represent a solution to the traveling salesman problem. However, because each city ID must appear in the encoding at least once, and only once, we looked at two new crossover and mutation methods that can keep to this constraint: ordered crossover and swap mutation.

In ordered crossover, a random subset of parent1's chromosome is added to the offspring, then the remaining genetic information needed is added to the offspring in the order it's found in parent2's chromosome. This method of adding a subset of parent1's genetic information, then only adding the missing remaining genetic information from parent2 guarantees each city ID will appear once and only once in the solution.

In swap mutation, two genes are selected and their positions are swapped. Again, this mutation method guarantees a valid solution for the traveling salesman problem, as it doesn't allow a city ID to be removed completely, nor can it cause a city to appear twice.

Exercises

1. Hard-code cities into the TSP class "main" method so that you can accurately take benchmarks of performance.

2. Add support for both, shortest route and quickest route using user defined distances and times between cities.

3. Add support for an asymmetric TSP (the cost of traveling from A to B may not equal the cost from traveling from B to A).

4. Modify the Individual class constructor to randomize the order of cities. How does this affect the performance of the algorithm?

5. Update the termination condition to measure the algorithm's progress and quit when no significant progress is being made. How does this affect the algorithm's performance and results?

Class Scheduling

Introduction

In this chapter, we will create a genetic algorithm that schedules classes for a college timetable. We will examine a couple of different scenarios in which a class-scheduling algorithm may be used, and the constraints that are usually implemented when designing a timetable. Finally, we will build a simple class scheduler, which can be expanded to support more complex implementations.

In artificial intelligence, *class scheduling* is a variation of the constraint satisfaction problem. This category of problem relates to problems, which have a set of variables that need to be assigned in such a way that they avoid violating a defined set of constraints.

Constraints fall into two categories: hard constraints—constraints which need to be satisfied to produce a functional solution, and soft constraints—constraints which are preferred but not at the expense of the hard constraints.

For instance, when manufacturing a new product, the product's functional requirements are hard constraints and specify the important performance requirements. Without these constraints, you have no product. A phone that can't make calls is hardly a phone! However, you may also have soft constraints, which, although unrequired, are still important to consider, such as the cost, weight, or aesthetics of the product.

When creating a class-scheduling algorithm there will typically be many hard and soft constraints that need to be considered. Some typical hard constraints for the class-scheduling problem are:

- Professors can only be in one class at any given time
- Classrooms need to be big enough to host the class
- Classrooms can only host one class at any given time
- Classrooms must contain any required equipment

Some typical soft constraints may be:

- Room capacity should be suitable for the class size
- Preferred classroom of the professor
- Preferred class time of the professor

Sometimes multiple soft constraints may conflict and a tradeoff will need to be found between them. For example, a class might only have 10 students so a soft constraint may reward assigning a suitable classroom, which has capacity of around 10; however, the professor taking the class may prefer a larger classroom, which can hold 30 students. If professor preferences are accounted for as soft constraints, one of these configurations will be preferred and hopefully found by the class scheduler.

In more advanced implementations it is also possible to weight soft constraints so the algorithm understands which soft constraints are the most important to consider.

Like the traveling salesman problem, iterative methods can be used to find an optimal solution to the class-scheduling problem; however, it becomes increasingly more difficult to find an optimal solution as the number of class configurations increases. In these circumstances, where the possible number of class configurations exceeds what is feasible to solve by iterative methods, genetic algorithms are good alternatives. Although they're not guaranteed to find the optimal solution, they are extremely good at finding close to optimal solutions within a reasonable timeframe.

The Problem

The class-scheduling problem we will be looking at in this chapter is a college class scheduler that can create a college timetable based on data we provide it, such as the available professors, available rooms, timeslots and student groups.

We should note that building a college timetable is slightly different from building a grade school timetable. Grade school timetables require their students to have a full timetable of scheduled classes throughout the day with no free periods. Conversely, typical college timetables will frequently have free periods depending on how many modules the student enrolls in.

Each class will be assigned a timeslot, a professor, a room and a student group by the class scheduler. We can calculate the total number of classes that will need scheduling by summing the number of student groups multiplied by the number of modules each student group is enrolled in.

For each class scheduled by our application we will consider the following hard constraints:

- Classes can only be scheduled in free classrooms
- A professor can only teach one class at any one time
- Classrooms must be big enough to accommodate the student group

To keep things simple in this implementation we will consider only hard constraints for now; however there would typically be many more hard constraints depending on the timetable specifications. There would also likely be a number of soft constraints included in the specification, which for now we will ignore. Although not necessary, considering soft constraints can often make a big difference in the quality of the timetables produced by the genetic algorithm.

Implementation

It is time to go ahead and tackle the problem using our knowledge of genetic algorithms. After setting up a new Java/Eclipse package for this problem, we'll begin by encoding the chromosome.

Before You Start

This chapter will build on the code you developed in all of the previous chapters – so it's especially important to follow this section closely!

Before you start, create a new Eclipse or NetBeans project, or create a new package in your existing project for this book called "chapter5".

Copy the Individual, Population, and GeneticAlgorithm classes over from chapter4 and import them into chapter5. Make sure to update the package name at the top of each class file! They should all say "package chapter5" at the very top.

Open the GeneticAlgorithm class and make the following changes:

- Delete the selectParent method, and replace it with the selectParent method from **chapter3** (tournament selection)

- Delete the crossoverPopulation method, and replace it with the crossoverPopulation method from **chapter2** (uniform crossover)

- Delete the initPopulation, mutatePopulation, evalPopulation, and calcPopulation methods – you'll re-implement them in this chapter

The Population and Individual classes can be left alone for now, but keep in mind that you'll be adding a new constructor to each one of these files later in the chapter.

Encoding

The encoding we use in our class scheduling application will need to be capable of efficiently encoding all of the class properties we require. For this implementation, they are: the timeslot the class is scheduled for, the professor teaching the class, and the classroom for the class.

We can simply assign a numerical ID to each timeslot, professor and classroom. We can then use a chromosome that encodes an array of integers—our familiar approach. This means each class that needs scheduling will only require three integers to encode it as shown below:

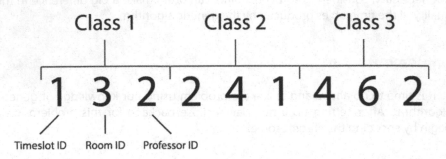

By splitting this array into chucks of three, we can retrieve all of the information we need for each class.

Initialization

Now that we have an understanding of our problem and how we're going to encode the chromosome, we can begin the implementation. First, we'll need to create some data for our scheduler to work with: in particular, the rooms, professors, timeslots, modules and student groups that we're trying to build a timetable around.

Usually this data comes from a database containing the complete course module and student data. However, for the purpose of this implementation we will create some hard-coded dummy data to work with.

Let's first set up our supporting Java classes. We'll create a container class for each of the data types above (room, class, group, professor, module, and timeslot). While each of these container classes is very simple—they mostly define some class properties, getters, and setters, with no real logic. We'll print each of them in turn here.

First, create a Room class that stores information about a classroom. As always, if using Eclipse, you can create this class using the File ➤ New ➤ Class menu option.

```java
package chapter5;
public class Room {
        private final int roomId;
        private final String roomNumber;
        private final int capacity;
```

```
public Room(int roomId, String roomNumber, int capacity) {
        this.roomId = roomId;
        this.roomNumber = roomNumber;
        this.capacity = capacity;
}

public int getRoomId() {
        return this.roomId;
}

public String getRoomNumber() {
        return this.roomNumber;
}

public int getRoomCapacity() {
        return this.capacity;
}
}
```

This class contains a constructor, which accepts a room ID, a room number and the room capacity. It also provides methods to get the room's properties.

Next, create a Timeslot class; the timeslot represents the day of week and time that a class takes place.

```
package chapter5;
public class Timeslot {
    private final int timeslotId;
    private final String timeslot;

    public Timeslot(int timeslotId, String timeslot){
        this.timeslotId = timeslotId;
        this.timeslot = timeslot;
    }

    public int getTimeslotId(){
        return this.timeslotId;
    }

    public String getTimeslot(){
        return this.timeslot;
    }
}
```

A timeslot can be created using the constructor and passing it a timeslot ID and the timeslot details as a string (the details might look like "Mon 9:00 – 10:00"). The class also contains getters to fetch the object's properties.

The third class to set up is the Professor class:

```java
package chapter5;
public class Professor {
    private final int professorId;
    private final String professorName;

    public Professor(int professorId, String professorName){
        this.professorId = professorId;
        this.professorName = professorName;
    }

    public int getProfessorId(){
        return this.professorId;
    }

    public String getProfessorName(){
        return this.professorName;
    }
}
```

The Professor class contains a constructor accepting a professor ID and professor name; it also contains getter methods to retrieve the professor's properties.

Next, add a Module class to store information about the course modules. A "module" is what some might call a "course", like "Calculus 101" or "American History 302", and like real-life courses, can have multiple sections and groups of students taking the course at different times of the week with different professors.

```java
package chapter5;
public class Module {
    private final int moduleId;
    private final String moduleCode;
    private final String module;
    private final int professorIds[];

    public Module(int moduleId, String moduleCode, String module,
    int professorIds[]){
        this.moduleId = moduleId;
        this.moduleCode = moduleCode;
        this.module = module;
        this.professorIds = professorIds;
    }

    public int getModuleId(){
        return this.moduleId;
    }
```

```
    public String getModuleCode(){
        return this.moduleCode;
    }

    public String getModuleName(){
        return this.module;
    }

    public int getRandomProfessorId(){
        int professorId = professorIds[(int) (professorIds.length *
        Math.random())];
        return professorId;
    }
}
```

This module class contains a constructor that accepts a module ID (numeric), module code (something like "CS101" or "Hist302"), module name and an array of professor IDs, which can teach the module. The module class also provides getter methods – and a method to select a random professor ID.

The next class needed is a Group class class, which holds information about student groups.

```
package chapter5;
public class Group {
private final int groupId;
    private final int groupSize;
    private final int moduleIds[];

    public Group(int groupId, int groupSize, int moduleIds[]){
        this.groupId = groupId;
        this.groupSize = groupSize;
        this.moduleIds = moduleIds;
    }

    public int getGroupId(){
        return this.groupId;
    }

    public int getGroupSize(){
        return this.groupSize;
    }

    public int[] getModuleIds(){
        return this.moduleIds;
    }
}
```

The group class constructor accepts a group ID, a group size, and the module IDs the group is taking. It also provides getter methods to fetch the group information.

Next, add a "Class" class. Understandably, the terminology here may be confusing throughout the chapter – therefore a capitalized "Class" will refer to this Java class that you're about to create, and we'll use the lowercase "class" to refer to any other Java class.

The Class class represents a combination of all of the above. It represents a student group taking a section of a module at a specific time, in a specific room, with a specific professor.

```java
package chapter5;

public class Class {
        private final int classId;
        private final int groupId;
        private final int moduleId;
        private int professorId;
        private int timeslotId;
        private int roomId;

        public Class(int classId, int groupId, int moduleId) {
                this.classId = classId;
                this.moduleId = moduleId;
                this.groupId = groupId;
        }

        public void addProfessor(int professorId) {
                this.professorId = professorId;
        }

        public void addTimeslot(int timeslotId) {
                this.timeslotId = timeslotId;
        }

        public void setRoomId(int roomId) {
                this.roomId = roomId;
        }

        public int getClassId() {
                return this.classId;
        }

        public int getGroupId() {
                return this.groupId;
        }
```

```
        public int getModuleId() {
                return this.moduleId;
        }

        public int getProfessorId() {
                return this.professorId;
        }

        public int getTimeslotId() {
                return this.timeslotId;
        }

        public int getRoomId() {
                return this.roomId;
        }
}
```

Now we can create a Timetable class to encapsulate all these objects into one single timetable object. The Timetable class is the most important class thus far, as it's the only class that understands how the different constraints are supposed to interact with one another.

The Timetable class also understands how to parse a chromosome and create a candidate Timetable to be evaluated and scored.

```
package chapter5;

import java.util.HashMap;

public class Timetable {
        private final HashMap<Integer, Room> rooms;
        private final HashMap<Integer, Professor> professors;
        private final HashMap<Integer, Module> modules;
        private final HashMap<Integer, Group> groups;
        private final HashMap<Integer, Timeslot> timeslots;
        private Class classes[];

        private int numClasses = 0;

        /**
         * Initialize new Timetable
         *
         */
        public Timetable() {
                this.rooms = new HashMap<Integer, Room>();
                this.professors = new HashMap<Integer, Professor>();
                this.modules = new HashMap<Integer, Module>();
```

```java
        this.groups = new HashMap<Integer, Group>();
        this.timeslots = new HashMap<Integer, Timeslot>();
}

public Timetable(Timetable cloneable) {
        this.rooms = cloneable.getRooms();
        this.professors = cloneable.getProfessors();
        this.modules = cloneable.getModules();
        this.groups = cloneable.getGroups();
        this.timeslots = cloneable.getTimeslots();
}

private HashMap<Integer, Group> getGroups() {
        return this.groups;
}

private HashMap<Integer, Timeslot> getTimeslots() {
        return this.timeslots;
}

private HashMap<Integer, Module> getModules() {
        return this.modules;
}

private HashMap<Integer, Professor> getProfessors() {
        return this.professors;
}

/**
 * Add new room
 *
 * @param roomId
 * @param roomName
 * @param capacity
 */
public void addRoom(int roomId, String roomName, int capacity) {
        this.rooms.put(roomId, new Room(roomId, roomName, capacity));
}

/**
 * Add new professor
 *
 * @param professorId
 * @param professorName
 */
```

```java
public void addProfessor(int professorId, String professorName) {
        this.professors.put(professorId, new Professor(professorId,
        professorName));
}

/**
 * Add new module
 *
 * @param moduleId
 * @param moduleCode
 * @param module
 * @param professorIds
 */
public void addModule(int moduleId, String moduleCode, String
        module, int professorIds[]) {
        this.modules.put(moduleId, new Module(moduleId, moduleCode,
        module, professorIds));
}

/**
 * Add new group
 *
 * @param groupId
 * @param groupSize
 * @param moduleIds
 */
public void addGroup(int groupId, int groupSize, int moduleIds[]) {
        this.groups.put(groupId, new Group(groupId, groupSize,
        moduleIds));
        this.numClasses = 0;
}

/**
 * Add new timeslot
 *
 * @param timeslotId
 * @param timeslot
 */
public void addTimeslot(int timeslotId, String timeslot) {
        this.timeslots.put(timeslotId, new Timeslot(timeslotId,
        timeslot));
}

/**
 * Create classes using individual's chromosome
 *
 * @param individual
 */
```

```java
public void createClasses(Individual individual) {
    // Init classes
    Class classes[] = new Class[this.getNumClasses()];

    // Get individual's chromosome
    int chromosome[] = individual.getChromosome();
    int chromosomePos = 0;
    int classIndex = 0;

    for (Group group : this.getGroupsAsArray()) {
        int moduleIds[] = group.getModuleIds();
        for (int moduleId : moduleIds) {
            classes[classIndex] = new Class(classIndex,
            group.getGroupId(), moduleId);

            // Add timeslot

            classes[classIndex].addTimeslot(chromosome
            [chromosomePos]);
            chromosomePos++;

            // Add room

            classes[classIndex].setRoomId(chromosome
            [chromosomePos]);
            chromosomePos++;

            // Add professor

            classes[classIndex].addProfessor(chromosome
            [chromosomePos]);
            chromosomePos++;

            classIndex++;
        }
    }

    this.classes = classes;
}

/**
 * Get room from roomId
 *
 * @param roomId
 * @return room
 */
```

```java
public Room getRoom(int roomId) {
        if (!this.rooms.containsKey(roomId)) {
                System.out.println("Rooms doesn't contain key " +
                roomId);
        }
        return (Room) this.rooms.get(roomId);
}

public HashMap<Integer, Room> getRooms() {
        return this.rooms;
}

/**
 * Get random room
 *
 * @return room
 */
public Room getRandomRoom() {
        Object[] roomsArray = this.rooms.values().toArray();
        Room room = (Room) roomsArray[(int) (roomsArray.length *
        Math.random())];
        return room;
}

/**
 * Get professor from professorId
 *
 * @param professorId
 * @return professor
 */
public Professor getProfessor(int professorId) {
        return (Professor) this.professors.get(professorId);
}

/**
 * Get module from moduleId
 *
 * @param moduleId
 * @return module
 */
public Module getModule(int moduleId) {
        return (Module) this.modules.get(moduleId);
}
```

```java
/**
 * Get moduleIds of student group
 *
 * @param groupId
 * @return moduleId array
 */
public int[] getGroupModules(int groupId) {
        Group group = (Group) this.groups.get(groupId);
        return group.getModuleIds();
}

/**
 * Get group from groupId
 *
 * @param groupId
 * @return group
 */
public Group getGroup(int groupId) {
        return (Group) this.groups.get(groupId);
}

/**
 * Get all student groups
 *
 * @return array of groups
 */
public Group[] getGroupsAsArray() {
        return (Group[]) this.groups.values().toArray(new
        Group[this.groups.size()]);
}

/**
 * Get timeslot by timeslotId
 *
 * @param timeslotId
 * @return timeslot
 */
public Timeslot getTimeslot(int timeslotId) {
        return (Timeslot) this.timeslots.get(timeslotId);
}

/**
 * Get random timeslotId
 *
 * @return timeslot
 */
```

```java
public Timeslot getRandomTimeslot() {
        Object[] timeslotArray = this.timeslots.values().toArray();
        Timeslot timeslot = (Timeslot) timeslotArray[(int)
        (timeslotArray.length * Math.random())];
        return timeslot;
}

/**
 * Get classes
 *
 * @return classes
 */
public Class[] getClasses() {
        return this.classes;
}

/**
 * Get number of classes that need scheduling
 *
 * @return numClasses
 */
public int getNumClasses() {
        if (this.numClasses > 0) {
                return this.numClasses;
        }

        int numClasses = 0;
        Group groups[] = (Group[]) this.groups.values().toArray(new
        Group[this.groups.size()]);
        for (Group group : groups) {
                numClasses += group.getModuleIds().length;
        }
        this.numClasses = numClasses;

        return this.numClasses;
}

/**
 * Calculate the number of clashes
 *
 * @return numClashes
 */
public int calcClashes() {
        int clashes = 0;
```

```
for (Class classA : this.classes) {
        // Check room capacity
        int roomCapacity = this.getRoom(classA.getRoomId()).
        getRoomCapacity();
        int groupSize = this.getGroup(classA.getGroupId()).
        getGroupSize();
        if (roomCapacity < groupSize) {
                clashes++;
        }

        // Check if room is taken
        for (Class classB : this.classes) {
                if (classA.getRoomId() == classB.getRoomId()
                && classA.getTimeslotId() == classB.
                getTimeslotId()
                                && classA.getClassId() !=
                                classB.getClassId()) {
                        clashes++;
                        break;
                }
        }

        // Check if professor is available
        for (Class classB : this.classes) {
                if (classA.getProfessorId() == classB.
                getProfessorId() && classA.getTimeslotId() ==
                classB.getTimeslotId()
                                && classA.getClassId() !=
                                classB.getClassId()) {
                        clashes++;
                        break;
                }
        }
}

return clashes;
    }
}
```

This class contains methods to add rooms, timeslots, professors, modules and groups to the timetable. In this manner, the Timetable class serves dual purposes: a Timetable object knows *all* of the *available* rooms, timeslots, professors, etc., but the Timetable object can *also* read a chromosome, create a subset of classes from that chromosome, and help evaluate the fitness of the chromosome.

Pay close attention to the two important methods in this class: createClasses and calcClashes.

The createClasses method accepts an Individual (that is, a chromosome) – and using its knowledge of the total number of student groups and modules that *must* be scheduled, creates a number of Class objects for those groups and modules. The method then starts reading the chromosome and assigns the variable information (a timeslot, a room, and a professor) to each one of those classes. Therefore, the createClasses method makes sure that every module and student group is accounted for, but it uses a genetic algorithm and the resultant chromosome to try different combinations of timeslots, rooms, and professors. The Timetable class caches this information locally (as "this.classes") for later use.

Once the Classes have been built, the calcClashes method checks each one in turn and counts the number of "clashes". In this case, a "clash" is any hard constraint violation, such as a class whose room is too small, a conflict with room and timeslot, or a conflict with professor and timeslot. The number of clashes is used later by the GeneticAlgorithm's calcFitness method.

The Executive Class

We can now create an executive class that contains the program's "main" method. As in previous chapters, we'll build this class based on the pseudocode from Chapter 2 with a number of "TODO" comments in place of the implementation details that we'll fill out throughout this chapter.

First, create a new Java class and call it "TimetableGA". Make sure it's in "package chapter5" and add the following code to it:

```java
package chapter5;

public class TimetableGA {

    public static void main(String[] args) {
        // TODO: Create Timetable and initialize with all the available
        courses, rooms, timeslots, professors, modules, and groups

        // Initialize GA
        GeneticAlgorithm ga = new GeneticAlgorithm(100, 0.01, 0.9, 2, 5);

        // TODO: Initialize population

        // TODO: Evaluate population

        // Keep track of current generation
        int generation = 1;
```

```
            // Start evolution loop
                // TODO: Add termination condition
            while (false) {
                // Print fitness
                System.out.println("G" + generation + " Best fitness: " +
                population.getFittest(0).getFitness());

                // Apply crossover
                population = ga.crossoverPopulation(population);

                // TODO: Apply mutation

                // TODO: Evaluate population

                // Increment the current generation
                generation++;
            }

            // TODO: Print final fitness

            // TODO: Print final timetable
    }
}
```

We've given ourselves eight TODOs in order to complete this chapter. Note that crossover is not a TODO we're reusing tournament selection from Chapter 3 with uniform crossover from Chapter 2.

The first TODO is easy to resolve, and we'll do that now. Generally, the information for a school's course scheduler will come from a database, but let's hard-code some classes and professors now. Since the following code is a little lengthy, let's create a separate method in the TimetableGA class for it. Add this method anywhere you like:

```
private static Timetable initializeTimetable() {
        // Create timetable
        Timetable timetable = new Timetable();

        // Set up rooms
        timetable.addRoom(1, "A1", 15);
        timetable.addRoom(2, "B1", 30);
        timetable.addRoom(4, "D1", 20);
        timetable.addRoom(5, "F1", 25);

        // Set up timeslots
        timetable.addTimeslot(1, "Mon 9:00 - 11:00");
        timetable.addTimeslot(2, "Mon 11:00 - 13:00");
        timetable.addTimeslot(3, "Mon 13:00 - 15:00");
```

```
    timetable.addTimeslot(4, "Tue 9:00 - 11:00");
    timetable.addTimeslot(5, "Tue 11:00 - 13:00");
    timetable.addTimeslot(6, "Tue 13:00 - 15:00");
    timetable.addTimeslot(7, "Wed 9:00 - 11:00");
    timetable.addTimeslot(8, "Wed 11:00 - 13:00");
    timetable.addTimeslot(9, "Wed 13:00 - 15:00");
    timetable.addTimeslot(10, "Thu 9:00 - 11:00");
    timetable.addTimeslot(11, "Thu 11:00 - 13:00");
    timetable.addTimeslot(12, "Thu 13:00 - 15:00");
    timetable.addTimeslot(13, "Fri 9:00 - 11:00");
    timetable.addTimeslot(14, "Fri 11:00 - 13:00");
    timetable.addTimeslot(15, "Fri 13:00 - 15:00");

    // Set up professors
    timetable.addProfessor(1, "Dr P Smith");
    timetable.addProfessor(2, "Mrs E Mitchell");
    timetable.addProfessor(3, "Dr R Williams");
    timetable.addProfessor(4, "Mr A Thompson");

    // Set up modules and define the professors that teach them
    timetable.addModule(1, "cs1", "Computer Science", new int[] { 1, 2 });
    timetable.addModule(2, "en1", "English", new int[] { 1, 3 });
    timetable.addModule(3, "ma1", "Maths", new int[] { 1, 2 });
    timetable.addModule(4, "ph1", "Physics", new int[] { 3, 4 });
    timetable.addModule(5, "hi1", "History", new int[] { 4 });
    timetable.addModule(6, "dr1", "Drama", new int[] { 1, 4 });

    // Set up student groups and the modules they take.
    timetable.addGroup(1, 10, new int[] { 1, 3, 4 });
    timetable.addGroup(2, 30, new int[] { 2, 3, 5, 6 });
    timetable.addGroup(3, 18, new int[] { 3, 4, 5 });
    timetable.addGroup(4, 25, new int[] { 1, 4 });
    timetable.addGroup(5, 20, new int[] { 2, 3, 5 });
    timetable.addGroup(6, 22, new int[] { 1, 4, 5 });
    timetable.addGroup(7, 16, new int[] { 1, 3 });
    timetable.addGroup(8, 18, new int[] { 2, 6 });
    timetable.addGroup(9, 24, new int[] { 1, 6 });
    timetable.addGroup(10, 25, new int[] { 3, 4 });
    return timetable;
}
```

Now, resolve the first TODO at the top of the main method by replacing it with the following:

```
// Get a Timetable object with all the available information.
Timetable timetable = initializeTimetable();
```

The top of the main method should now look like this:

```
public class TimetableGA {

    public static void main(String[] args) {
        // Get a Timetable object with all the available information.
        Timetable timetable = initializeTimetable();

        // Initialize GA ... (and the rest of the class, unchanged
        from before!)
        GeneticAlgorithm ga = new GeneticAlgorithm(100, 0.01, 0.9, 2, 5);
```

This gives us a Timetable instance with all of the necessary information, and the GeneticAlgorithm object we create is similar to those in previous chapters: a genetic algorithm with a population of 100, a mutation rate of 0.01, a crossover rate of 0.9, 2 elite individuals and a tournament size of 5.

We now have seven TODOs remaining. The next TODO is related to initializing a population. In order to create a population, we'll need to know the length of the chromosome we need; and that's determined by the number of groups and modules in the Timetable.

We need to be able to initialize a Population from a Timetable object, which means that we also need to be able to initialize an Individual from a Timetable object. In order to resolve this TODO, therefore, we must do three things: add an initPopulation(Timetable) method to the GeneticAlgorithm class, add a constructor to Population that accepts a Timetable, and add a constructor to Individual that accepts a Timetable.

Let's start from the bottom and work our way up. Update the Individual class by adding a new constructor that builds an Individual from a Timetable. The constructor uses the Timetable object to determine the number of classes that must be scheduled, which dictates the chromosome length. The chromosome itself is built by taking random rooms, timeslots, and professors from the Timetable.

Add the following method to the Individual class, anywhere you like:

```
public Individual(Timetable timetable) {
    int numClasses = timetable.getNumClasses();

    // 1 gene for room, 1 for time, 1 for professor
    int chromosomeLength = numClasses * 3;
    // Create random individual
    int newChromosome[] = new int[chromosomeLength];
    int chromosomeIndex = 0;
    // Loop through groups
    for (Group group : timetable.getGroupsAsArray()) {
        // Loop through modules
```

```
for (int moduleId : group.getModuleIds()) {
    // Add random time
    int timeslotId = timetable.getRandomTimeslot().
    getTimeslotId();
    newChromosome[chromosomeIndex] = timeslotId;
    chromosomeIndex++;

    // Add random room
    int roomId = timetable.getRandomRoom().getRoomId();
    newChromosome[chromosomeIndex] = roomId;
    chromosomeIndex++;

    // Add random professor
    Module module = timetable.getModule(moduleId);
    newChromosome[chromosomeIndex] = module.
    getRandomProfessorId();
    chromosomeIndex++;
    }
}

this.chromosome = newChromosome;
}
```

This constructor accepts a timetable object and loops over each student group and each module the group is enrolled in (giving us the total number of Classes that need scheduling). For each Class a random room, professor, and timeslot is selected and the corresponding ID is added to the chromosome.

Next, add this constructor method to the Population class. This constructor builds a Population from Individuals initialized with the Timetable, by simply calling the Individual constructor we just created.

```
public Population(int populationSize, Timetable timetable) {
    // Initial population
    this.population = new Individual[populationSize];

    // Loop over population size
    for (int individualCount = 0; individualCount < populationSize;
    individualCount++) {
        // Create individual
        Individual individual = new Individual(timetable);
        // Add individual to population
        this.population[individualCount] = individual;
    }
}
```

Next, re-implement the initPopulation method in the GeneticAlgorithm class to use the new Population constructor:

```java
public Population initPopulation(Timetable timetable) {
        // Initialize population
        Population population = new Population(this.populationSize, timetable);
        return population;
}
```

We can finally resolve our next TODO: replace "TODO: Initialize Population" in the executive class' main method and invoke the GeneticAlgorithm's initPopulation method:

```java
        // Initialize population
        Population population = ga.initPopulation(timetable);
```

The main method of the executive TimetableGA class should now look like the following. Since we haven't implemented a termination condition, this code won't do anything interesting yet, In fact the Java compiler may complain about unreachable code inside the loop. We'll fix this shortly.

```java
public static void main(String[] args) {
        // Get a Timetable object with all the available information.
        Timetable timetable = initializeTimetable();

        // Initialize GA
        GeneticAlgorithm ga = new GeneticAlgorithm(100, 0.01, 0.9, 2, 5);

        // Initialize population
        Population population = ga.initPopulation(timetable);

        // TODO: Evaluate population

        // Keep track of current generation
        int generation = 1;

        // Start evolution loop
        // TODO: Add termination condition
        while (false) {
                // Print fitness
                System.out.println("G" + generation + " Best fitness: " +
                population.getFittest(0).getFitness());

                // Apply crossover
                population = ga.crossoverPopulation(population);
```

```
        // TODO: Apply mutation

        // TODO: Evaluate population

        // Increment the current generation
        generation++;
    }

    // TODO: Print final fitness

    // TODO: Print final timetable
}
```

Evaluation

Our initial population has been created, and we need to evaluate those individuals and assign them fitness values. We know from earlier that the goal is to optimize our class timetable in a way that will avoid breaking as many constraints as possible. This means an individual's fitness value will be inversely proportional to how many constraints it violates.

Open up and inspect the Timetable class' "createClasses" method. Using its knowledge of all the Groups and Modules that need to be scheduled into classrooms with professors at specific times, it transforms a chromosome into an array of Class objects and stashes them away for evaluation. This method doesn't do any actual evaluation, but it is the bridge between a chromosome and the evaluation step.

Next, inspect the "calcClashes" method in the same class. This method compares each class to every other class and adds a "clash" if any hard constraints are violated, for instance: if the selected room is too small, if there's a scheduling conflict for the room, or if there's a scheduling conflict for the professor. The method returns the total number of clashes it found.

Now we have everything in place to create our fitness function and finally to evaluate the fitnesses of the individuals in our population.

Open the GeneticAlgorithm class and first add the following calcFitness method.

```
public double calcFitness(Individual individual, Timetable timetable) {

        // Create new timetable object to use -- cloned from an existing
        timetable
        Timetable threadTimetable = new Timetable(timetable);
        threadTimetable.createClasses(individual);

        // Calculate fitness
        int clashes = threadTimetable.calcClashes();
        double fitness = 1 / (double) (clashes + 1);
```

```
        individual.setFitness(fitness);

        return fitness;
}
```

The calcFitness method clones the Timetable object given to it, calls the createClasses method, and then calculates the number of clashes via the calcClashes method. The fitness is defined as the inverse as the number of clashes—0 clashes will result in a fitness of 1.

Add an evalPopulation method to the GeneticAlgorithm class as well. As in previous chapters, this method simply iterates through the population and calls calcFitness for each.

```
public void evalPopulation(Population population, Timetable timetable) {
        double populationFitness = 0;

        // Loop over population evaluating individuals and summing
        population
        // fitness
        for (Individual individual : population.getIndividuals()) {
                populationFitness += this.calcFitness(individual, timetable);
        }

        population.setPopulationFitness(populationFitness);
}
```

Finally, we can evaluate the population and resolve some TODOs in the executive TimetableGA class' main method. Update the **two** locations that have "TODO: Evaluate Population" to instead show:

```
// Evaluate population
ga.evalPopulation(population, timetable);
```

At this point, there should be four TODOs remaining. The program is still not runnable at this point, because the termination condition hasn't been defined and the loop hasn't yet been enabled.

Termination

Our next step in building our class scheduler is to set up a termination check. Previously, we have used both the number of generations and the fitness to decide whether we want to terminate our genetic algorithm. This time we will combine both of these termination conditions, terminating our genetic algorithm either after a certain number of generations have past, or if it finds a valid solution.

Because the fitness value is based on the number of broken constraints, we know that a perfect solution will have a fitness value of 1. Leave the previous termination check intact, and add this second termination check to the GeneticAlgorithm class. We'll use both checks in our executive loop.

```
public boolean isTerminationConditionMet(Population population) {
        return population.getFittest(0).getFitness() == 1.0;
}
```

At this point, confirm that the second isTerminationConditionMet method (which should already be in the GeneticAlgorithm class) looks like the following:

```
public boolean isTerminationConditionMet(int generationsCount, int
maxGenerations) {
        return (generationsCount > maxGenerations);
}
```

Now we can add our two termination checks to our main method and enable the evolution loop. Open up the executive TimetableGA class, and resolve the "TODO: Add termination condition" TODO as follows:

```
// Start evolution loop
while (ga.isTerminationConditionMet(generation, 1000) == false
        && ga.isTerminationConditionMet(population) == false) {

        // Rest of the loop in here...
```

The first isTerminationConditionMet call limits us to 1,000 generations, while the second checks to see if there are any individuals with a fitness of 1 in the population.

Let's resolve two more TODOs very quickly. We have some simple reporting to present when the loop ends. Delete the two TODOs after the loop ("Print final fitness" and "Print final timetable") and replace them with the following:

```
// Print fitness
timetable.createClasses(population.getFittest(0));
System.out.println();
System.out.println("Solution found in " + generation + " generations");
System.out.println("Final solution fitness: " + population.getFittest(0).
getFitness());
System.out.println("Clashes: " + timetable.calcClashes());

// Print classes
System.out.println();
Class classes[] = timetable.getClasses();
int classIndex = 1;
```

```
for (Class bestClass : classes) {
    System.out.println("Class " + classIndex + ":");
    System.out.println("Module: " +
timetable.getModule(bestClass.getModuleId()).getModuleName());
    System.out.println("Group: " +
timetable.getGroup(bestClass.getGroupId()).getGroupId());
    System.out.println("Room: " +
timetable.getRoom(bestClass.getRoomId()).getRoomNumber());
    System.out.println("Professor: " +
timetable.getProfessor(bestClass.getProfessorId()).getProfessorName());
    System.out.println("Time: " +
timetable.getTimeslot(bestClass.getTimeslotId()).getTimeslot());
    System.out.println("-----");
    classIndex++;
}
```

At this point, you should be able to run the program, watch the evolution loop, and get a result. Without mutation, you may never find a solution, but the existing crossover methods that we repurposed from Chapters 2 and 3 are often sufficient to find a solution. However, if you run the program a number of times and you *never* reach a solution in less than 1,000 generations, you may want to re-read this chapter and make sure you haven't made any mistakes.

We leave the familiar "Crossover" section out of this chapter, as there are no new techniques to present here. Recall that uniform crossover from Chapter 2 selects chromosomes at random and swaps them with a parent, without preserving any continuity within groups of genes. This is a good approach for this problem, given that groups of genes (representing professor, room, and timeslot combinations) are more likely to be harmful than helpful in this case.

Mutation

Recall that constraints upon the chromosome often dictate the mutation and crossover techniques one selects for a genetic algorithm. In this case, a chromosome is built of specific room, professor, and timeslot IDs; we can not simply select random numbers. Additionally, since the rooms, professors, and timeslots all have a different range of IDs, we also can not simply choose a random number between 1 and "X". Potentially, we could choose random numbers for each of the different types of objects we're encoding (room, professor, and timeslot), but that also assumes that IDs are contiguous, and they may not be!

We can take a tip from uniform crossover to solve our mutation problem. In uniform crossover, genes are selected at random from an existing and valid parent. The parent might not be the fittest individual in the population, but at least it's valid.

Mutation can be implemented in a similar manner. Instead of choosing a random number for a random gene in the chromosome, we can create a new *random but valid individual* and essentially run uniform crossover to achieve mutation! That is, we can use our Individual(Timetable) constructor to create a brand new random Individual, and then select genes from the random Individual to copy into the Individual to be mutated. This technique is called *uniform mutation*, and makes sure that all of our mutated individuals are fully valid, never selecting a gene that doesn't make sense. Add the following method anywhere in the GeneticAlgorithm class:

```
public Population mutatePopulation(Population population, Timetable
timetable) {
    // Initialize new population
    Population newPopulation = new Population(this.populationSize);

    // Loop over current population by fitness
    for (int populationIndex = 0; populationIndex < population.size();
    populationIndex++) {
        Individual individual = population.
        getFittest(populationIndex);

        // Create random individual to swap genes with
        Individual randomIndividual = new Individual(timetable);

        // Loop over individual's genes
        for (int geneIndex = 0; geneIndex < individual.
        getChromosomeLength(); geneIndex++) {
            // Skip mutation if this is an elite individual
            if (populationIndex > this.elitismCount) {
                // Does this gene need mutation?
                if (this.mutationRate > Math.random()) {
                    // Swap for new gene
                    individual.setGene(geneIndex,
                    randomIndividual.getGene(geneIndex));
                }
            }
        }

        // Add individual to population
        newPopulation.setIndividual(populationIndex, individual);
    }

    // Return mutated population
    return newPopulation;
}
```

In this method, like mutations in previous chapters, the population is mutated by looping over the population's non-elite individuals. Unlike other mutation techniques which tend to modify genes directly, this mutation algorithm creates a random but valid individual and copies genes at random from that.

We can now resolve the final TODO in our executive class' main method. Add this one-liner to the main loop:

```
// Apply mutation
population = ga.mutatePopulation(population, timetable);
```

We should now have everything in place to run our genetic algorithm and create a new college timetable. If your Java IDE is showing errors, or if it won't compile at this point, please go back through this chapter and resolve any issues you find.

Execution

Make sure your TimetableGA class looks like the following:

```
package chapter5;

public class TimetableGA {

    public static void main(String[] args) {
        // Get a Timetable object with all the available information.
        Timetable timetable = initializeTimetable();

        // Initialize GA
        GeneticAlgorithm ga = new GeneticAlgorithm(100, 0.01, 0.9, 2, 5);

        // Initialize population
        Population population = ga.initPopulation(timetable);

        // Evaluate population
        ga.evalPopulation(population, timetable);

        // Keep track of current generation
        int generation = 1;

        // Start evolution loop
        while (ga.isTerminationConditionMet(generation, 1000) == false
            && ga.isTerminationConditionMet(population) == false) {
            // Print fitness
            System.out.println("G" + generation + " Best fitness: " +
            population.getFittest(0).getFitness());
```

```
        // Apply crossover
        population = ga.crossoverPopulation(population);

        // Apply mutation
        population = ga.mutatePopulation(population, timetable);

        // Evaluate population
        ga.evalPopulation(population, timetable);

        // Increment the current generation
        generation++;
    }

    // Print fitness
    timetable.createClasses(population.getFittest(0));
    System.out.println();
    System.out.println("Solution found in " + generation + "
    generations");
    System.out.println("Final solution fitness: " + population.
    getFittest(0).getFitness());
    System.out.println("Clashes: " + timetable.calcClashes());

    // Print classes
    System.out.println();
    Class classes[] = timetable.getClasses();
    int classIndex = 1;
    for (Class bestClass : classes) {
        System.out.println("Class " + classIndex + ":");
        System.out.println("Module: " +
                timetable.getModule(bestClass.getModuleId()).
                getModuleName());
        System.out.println("Group: " +
                timetable.getGroup(bestClass.getGroupId()).
                getGroupId());
        System.out.println("Room: " +
                timetable.getRoom(bestClass.getRoomId()).
                getRoomNumber());
        System.out.println("Professor: " +
                timetable.getProfessor(bestClass.getProfessorId()).
                getProfessorName());
        System.out.println("Time: " +
                timetable.getTimeslot(bestClass.getTimeslotId()).
                getTimeslot());
        System.out.println("-----");
        classIndex++;
    }
}
```

```java
/**
 * Creates a Timetable with all the necessary course information.
 * @return
 */
  private static Timetable initializeTimetable() {
        // Create timetable
        Timetable timetable = new Timetable();

        // Set up rooms
        timetable.addRoom(1, "A1", 15);
        timetable.addRoom(2, "B1", 30);
        timetable.addRoom(4, "D1", 20);
        timetable.addRoom(5, "F1", 25);

        // Set up timeslots
        timetable.addTimeslot(1, "Mon 9:00 - 11:00");
        timetable.addTimeslot(2, "Mon 11:00 - 13:00");
        timetable.addTimeslot(3, "Mon 13:00 - 15:00");
        timetable.addTimeslot(4, "Tue 9:00 - 11:00");
        timetable.addTimeslot(5, "Tue 11:00 - 13:00");
        timetable.addTimeslot(6, "Tue 13:00 - 15:00");
        timetable.addTimeslot(7, "Wed 9:00 - 11:00");
        timetable.addTimeslot(8, "Wed 11:00 - 13:00");
        timetable.addTimeslot(9, "Wed 13:00 - 15:00");
        timetable.addTimeslot(10, "Thu 9:00 - 11:00");
        timetable.addTimeslot(11, "Thu 11:00 - 13:00");
        timetable.addTimeslot(12, "Thu 13:00 - 15:00");
        timetable.addTimeslot(13, "Fri 9:00 - 11:00");
        timetable.addTimeslot(14, "Fri 11:00 - 13:00");
        timetable.addTimeslot(15, "Fri 13:00 - 15:00");

        // Set up professors
        timetable.addProfessor(1, "Dr P Smith");
        timetable.addProfessor(2, "Mrs E Mitchell");
        timetable.addProfessor(3, "Dr R Williams");
        timetable.addProfessor(4, "Mr A Thompson");

        // Set up modules and define the professors that teach them
        timetable.addModule(1, "cs1", "Computer Science",
        new int[] { 1, 2 });
        timetable.addModule(2, "en1", "English", new int[] { 1, 3 });
        timetable.addModule(3, "ma1", "Maths", new int[] { 1, 2 });
        timetable.addModule(4, "ph1", "Physics", new int[] { 3, 4 });
        timetable.addModule(5, "hi1", "History", new int[] { 4 });
        timetable.addModule(6, "dr1", "Drama", new int[] { 1, 4 });
```

```
            // Set up student groups and the modules they take.
            timetable.addGroup(1, 10, new int[] { 1, 3, 4 });
            timetable.addGroup(2, 30, new int[] { 2, 3, 5, 6 });
            timetable.addGroup(3, 18, new int[] { 3, 4, 5 });
            timetable.addGroup(4, 25, new int[] { 1, 4 });
            timetable.addGroup(5, 20, new int[] { 2, 3, 5 });
            timetable.addGroup(6, 22, new int[] { 1, 4, 5 });
            timetable.addGroup(7, 16, new int[] { 1, 3 });
            timetable.addGroup(8, 18, new int[] { 2, 6 });
            timetable.addGroup(9, 24, new int[] { 1, 6 });
            timetable.addGroup(10, 25, new int[] { 3, 4 });
            return timetable;
        }
}
```

Running the class scheduler as-is should generate a solution in approximately 50 generations, and in all cases should present a solution with zero clashes (hard constraints). If your algorithm repeatedly hits the 1,000 generation limit, or if it presents solutions with clashes, there's likely something wrong with your implementation!

Take a minute to visually inspect the timetable results that the algorithm returns. Confirm that there are no actual clashes between professors, rooms, and timeslots.

At this point, you may also want to play with adding more professors, modules, timeslots, groups and rooms to the Timetable initialization in TimetableGA's "initializeTimetable" method. Can you force the algorithm to fail?

Analysis and Refinement

The class-scheduling problem is a good example of using genetic algorithms to search a solution space for valid solutions rather than optimal solutions. This problem can have many solutions with a fitness of 1, and all we need to do is find just one of those valid solutions. When considering only hard constraints, there's no real difference between any two valid solutions, and we can choose simply the first solution we find.

Unlike the traveling salesman problem from Chapter 4, this property of the class-scheduling problem means the algorithm can actually return invalid solutions. A solution in the traveling salesman problem can be invalid if it doesn't visit each city once, but because we took great care to design our initialization, crossover, and mutation algorithms, we won't ever encounter an invalid solution using the code from Chapter 4. All of the routes returned by our TSP solver are valid, and it's just a matter of finding the shortest possible route. If we stop the TSP algorithm at any point, during any generation, and pick a member of the population at random, it will be a valid solution.

In this chapter, however, *most* solutions are invalid and we stop only when we find the first valid solution or run out of time. The difference between the two problems is as follows: in the traveling salesman problem, it's easy to create a valid solution (just ensure every city is visited once; no guarantees as to the solution's fitness, though!), but in the class scheduler, creating a valid solution *is* the difficult part.

Additionally, without any soft constraints, there's no difference in fitness between any two valid solutions returned by the class scheduler. In this context, hard constraints determine whether a solution is valid, but soft constraints determine a solution's *quality*. The implementation above does not prefer any particular valid solution, because it has no means of determining the quality of a solution—it only knows if a solution is valid or not.

Adding soft constraints to the class scheduler changes the problem significantly. No longer are we searching for just any valid solution, but we want *the best* valid solution.

Fortunately, genetic algorithms are particularly good at this type of constraint juggling. The fact that an individual is judged only by a single number—its fitness—works to our advantage. The algorithm that determines an individual's fitness is completely opaque to the genetic algorithm—it's a black box as far as the genetic algorithm is concerned. While the fitness score is massively important to the genetic algorithm and can't be implemented haphazardly, its simplicity and opaqueness also lets us use it to reconcile all sorts of constraints and conditions. Because everything boils down to a single non-dimensional fitness score, we are able to scale and transform as many constraints as we like, and the importance of that constraint is represented by how strongly it contributes to the fitness score.

The class scheduler implemented above uses only hard constraints and confines the fitness score to the range 0-1. When combining different types of constraints, one should make sure that hard constraints have an overwhelming effect on the fitness score, while soft constraints make a more modest contribution.

As an example, imagine you needed to add a handful of soft constraints to the class scheduler, each with a slightly different importance. The hard constraints still apply, of course. How do you reconcile soft constraints with hard constraints? The existing fitness score of "1 / (clashes + 1)" clearly does not incorporate soft constraints—and even if it considered a broken soft constraint a "clash", would still put them all on equal footing with hard constraints. Under that model, it's possible to select an invalid solution because it may have a number of satisfied soft constraints that make up for the lost fitness caused by the broken hard constraint.

Instead, consider a new fitness scoring system: each broken hard constraint subtracts 100 from the fitness score, while any satisfied soft constraint may add 1, 2, or 3 points to the fitness score depending on its importance. Under this scheme, we should only consider solutions with a score of zero or above, as anything negative has a broken hard constraint. This scheme also ensures that there's no way a broken hard constraint can be canceled out by a large number of satisfied soft constraints – the contribution of a hard constraint to the fitness score is so overwhelming that there's no way the soft constraints can make up the 100 points penalized by a broken hard constraint. Finally, this scheme also allows you to prioritize the soft constraints—more important constraints can contribute more to the fitness score.

To further illustrate the idea that the fitness score normalizes constraints; consider any mapping and directions tool (like Google Maps). When you search for directions between two locations, the primary contributor to the fitness score is the amount of time it takes to get from place to place. A simple algorithm might use travel time in minutes as its fitness score (in this case, we'll call it "cost score", since lower is better, and the inverse of fitness is generally called "cost").

A route that takes 60 minutes is better than a route that takes 70 minutes – but we know that's not always the case in real life. Perhaps the shorter route has an exorbitant toll of $20. The user may choose the "Avoid Tolls" option, and now the algorithm has to reconcile driving minutes versus toll dollars. How many minutes is a dollar worth? If you decide that each dollar adds one point to the cost score, the shorter route now has a cost of 80, and loses to the longer but cheaper route. On the other hand, if you weigh toll-avoidance less and decide that one dollar of toll only adds a cost of 0.25 to the route, the shorter route will still win with a cost of 65.

Ultimately, when working with hard and soft constraints in genetic algorithms, be sure to understand what the fitness score represents and how each constraint will affect an individual's score.

Exercises

1. Add soft constraints to the class scheduler. This could include preferred professor time and preferred classrooms.

2. Implement support for a config file or database connection to add initial timetable data.

3. Build a class scheduler for a school timetable that requires students to have a class scheduled for each period.

Summary

In this chapter, we have covered the basics of class scheduling using genetic algorithms. Rather than using a genetic algorithm to find an *optimal* solution, we used a genetic algorithm to find the *first valid* solution that satisfies a number of hard constraints.

We also explored a new mutation tactic that ensures mutated chromosomes remain valid. Instead of modifying the chromosome directly and adding randomness—which may have led to invalid chromosomes in this case—we created a known-valid random Individual and swapped genes with it in a style reminiscent to uniform crossover. This algorithm is still considered uniform mutation, however the new approach used in this chapter made it easier to ensure valid mutation.

We also combined uniform crossover from Chapter 2 with tournament selection from Chapter 3, showing that many aspects of genetic algorithms are modular, independent, and able to be combined in different ways.

Finally, we discussed the flexibility of the fitness score in genetic algorithms. We learned that the non-dimensional fitness score can be used to introduce soft constraints and reconcile them with hard constraints, with the ultimate goal of producing not just valid results, but high-quality results as well.

Optimization   Chapter 6

In this chapter we will explore different techniques that are frequently used to optimize genetic algorithms. Additional optimization techniques become increasingly important as the problem being solved becomes more complex. A well-optimized algorithm can save hours or even days when solving larger problems; for this reason, optimization techniques are essential when the problem reaches a certain level of complexity.

In addition to exploring some common optimization techniques, this chapter will also cover a few implementation examples using the genetic algorithms from the previous chapters' case studies.

Adaptive Genetic Algorithms

Adaptive genetic algorithms (AGA) are a popular subset of genetic algorithms which can provide significant performance improvements over standard implementations when used in the right circumstances. As we have come to learn in the previous chapters, a key factor which determines how well a genetic algorithm will perform is the way in which its parameters are configured. We have already discussed the importance of finding the right values for the mutation rate and crossover rate when constructing an efficient genetic algorithm. Typically, configuring the parameters will require some trial and error, together with some intuition, before eventually reaching a satisfactory configuration. Adaptive genetic algorithms are useful because they can assist in the tuning of these parameters automatically by adjusting them based on the state of the algorithm. These parameter adjustments take place while the genetic algorithm is running, hopefully resulting in the best parameters being used at any specific time during execution. It's this continuous adaptive adjustment of the algorithm's parameters which will often result in a performance improvement for the genetic algorithm.

Adaptive genetic algorithms use information such as the average population fitness and the population's current best fitness to calculate and update its parameters in a way that best suits its present state. For example, by comparing any specific individual to the current fittest individual in the population, it's possible to gauge how well that individual is performing in relation to the current best. Typically, we want to increase the chance of preserving individuals that are performing well and reduce the chance of preserving individuals that don't perform well. One way we can do this is by allowing the algorithm to adaptively update the mutation rate.

Unfortunately, it's not quite that simple. After a while, the population will start to converge and individuals will begin to fall nearer to a single point in the search space. When this happens, the progress of the search can stall as there is very little difference between individuals. In this event, it can be effective to raise the mutation rate slightly, encouraging the search of alternative areas within the search space.

We can determine if the algorithm has begun to converge by calculating the difference between the current best fitness and the average population fitness. When the average population fitness is close to the current best fitness, we know the population has started to converge around a small area of the search space.

Adaptive genetic algorithms can be used to adjust more than just the mutation rate however. Similar techniques can be applied to adjust other parameters of the genetic algorithm such as the crossover rate to provide further improvements as needed.

Implementation

As with many things concerning genetic algorithms, the optimal way to update the parameters usually requires some experimentation. We will explore one of the more common approaches and leave it to you personally to experiment with other approaches if you wish.

As discussed previously, when calculating what the mutation rate should be for any given individual, two of the most important characteristics to consider are how well the current individual is performing and how well the entire population is performing as a whole. The algorithm we will use to assess these two characteristics and update the mutation rate is as follows:

$$p_m = (f_{max} - f_i) / (f_{max} - f_{avg}) * m, f_i > f_{avg}$$

$$p_m = m, f_i \leq f_{avg}$$

When the individual's fitness is greater than the population's average fitness we take the best fitness from the population (f_{max}) and find the difference between the current individual's fitness (f_i). We then find the difference between the max population fitness and the average population fitness (f_{avg}) and divide the two values. We can use this value to scale our mutation rate that was set during initialization. If the individual's fitness is the same or less than the population's average fitness we simply use the mutation rate as set during initialization.

To make things easier, we can implement our new adaptive genetic algorithm code into our previous class scheduler code. To begin, we need to add a new method for getting the average fitness of the population. We can do this by adding the following method to the Population class, anywhere in the file:

```
/**
 * Get average fitness
 *
 * @return The average individual fitness
 */
public double getAvgFitness(){
    if (this.populationFitness == -1) {
        double totalFitness = 0;
        for (Individual individual : population) {
            totalFitness += individual.getFitness();
        }

        this.populationFitness = totalFitness;
    }

    return populationFitness / this.size();
}
```

Now we can complete the implementation by updating the mutation function to use our adaptive mutation algorithm,

```
/**
 * Apply mutation to population
 *
 * @param population
 * @param timetable
 * @return The mutated population
 */
public Population mutatePopulation(Population population, Timetable
timetable){
    // Initialize new population
    Population newPopulation = new Population(this.populationSize);

    // Get best fitness
    double bestFitness = population.getFittest(0).getFitness();

    // Loop over current population by fitness
    for (int populationIndex = 0; populationIndex < population.size();
    populationIndex++) {
        Individual individual = population.getFittest(populationIndex);

        // Create random individual to swap genes with
        Individual randomIndividual = new Individual(timetable);
```

```
            // Calculate adaptive mutation rate
            double adaptiveMutationRate = this.mutationRate;
            if (individual.getFitness() > population.getAvgFitness()) {
                double fitnessDelta1 = bestFitness - individual.
                getFitness();
                double fitnessDelta2 = bestFitness - population.
                getAvgFitness();
                adaptiveMutationRate = (fitnessDelta1 / fitnessDelta2) *
                this.mutationRate;
            }

            // Loop over individual's genes
            for (int geneIndex = 0; geneIndex < individual.
            getChromosomeLength(); geneIndex++) {
                // Skip mutation if this is an elite individual
                if (populationIndex > this.elitismCount) {
                    // Does this gene need mutating?
                    if (adaptiveMutationRate > Math.random()) {
                        // Swap for new gene
                        individual.setGene(geneIndex, randomIndividual.
                        getGene(geneIndex));
                    }
                }
            }

            // Add individual to population
            newPopulation.setIndividual(populationIndex, individual);
        }

        // Return mutated population
        return newPopulation;
    }
```

This new mutatePopulation method is identical to the original except for the adaptive mutation code which implements the algorithm mentioned above.

When initializing the genetic algorithm with adaptive mutation enabled, the mutation rate used will now be the maximum possible mutation rate and will scale down depending on the fitness of the current individual and population as a whole. Because of this, a higher initial mutation rate may be beneficial.

Exercises

1. Use what you know about the adaptive mutation rate to implement an adaptive crossover rate into your genetic algorithm.

Multi-Heuristics

When it comes to optimizing genetic algorithms implementing a secondary heuristic is another common method to achieve significant performance improvements under certain conditions. Implementing a second heuristic into a genetic algorithm allows us to combine the best aspects of multiple heuristic approaches into one algorithm, providing further control over the search strategy and performance.

Two popular heuristics that are often implemented into genetic algorithms are simulated annealing and Tabu search. *Simulated annealing* is a search heuristic modeled on the process of annealing found in metallurgy. Put simply, it is a hill climbing algorithm that is designed to gradually reduce the rate in which worse solutions are accepted. In the context of genetic algorithms, simulated annealing will reduce the mutation rate and/or crossover rate over time.

On the other hand, *Tabu search* is a search algorithm that keeps a list of "tabu" (which derives from "taboo") solutions that prevents the algorithm from returning to previously visited areas in the search space that are known to be weak. This tabu list helps the algorithm avoid repeatedly considering solutions it's previously found and knows to be weak.

Typically, a multi-heuristic approach would only be implemented in situations where including it could bring certain needed improvements to the search process. For example, if the genetic algorithm is converging on an area in the search space too quickly, implementing simulated annealing into the algorithm might help to control how soon the algorithm converges.

Implementation

Let's go over a quick example of a multi-heuristic algorithm by combining the simulated annealing algorithm with a genetic algorithm. As mentioned previously, the simulated annealing algorithm is a hill climbing algorithm which initially accepts worse solutions at a high rate; then as the algorithm runs, it gradually reduces the rate in which worse solutions are accepted.

One of the easiest ways to implement this characteristic into a genetic algorithm is by updating the mutation and crossover rate to start with a high rate then gradually lower the rate of mutation and crossover as the algorithm progresses. This initial high mutation and crossover rate will cause the genetic algorithm to search a large area of the search space. Then as the mutation and crossover rate is slowly decreased the genetic algorithm should begin to focus its search on areas of the search space where fitness values are higher.

To vary the mutation and crossover probability, we use a temperature variable which starts high, or "hot", and slowly decreases, or "cools" as the algorithm runs. This heating and cooling technique is directly inspired by the process of annealing found in metallurgy. After each generation the temperature is cooled slightly, which decreases the mutation and crossover probability.

To begin the implementation, we need to create two new variables in the GeneticAlgorithm class. The coolingRate should be set to a small fraction, typically on the order of 0.001 or less – though this number will depend on the number of generations you expect to run and how aggressive you'd like the simulated annealing to be.

```
private double temperature = 1.0;
private double coolingRate;
```

Next, we need to create a function to cool the temperature based on the cooling rate.

```
/**
 * Cool temperature
 */
 public void coolTemperature() {
     this.temperature *= (1 - this.coolingRate);
 }
```

Now, we can update the mutation function to consider the temperature variable when deciding whether to apply mutation. We can do this by changing this line of code,

```
// Does this gene need mutation?
if (this.mutationRate > Math.random()) {
```

To now include the new temperature variable,

```
// Does this gene need mutation?
if ((this.mutationRate * this.getTempature()) > Math.random()) {
```

To finish this off, update the genetic algorithm's loop code in the executive class' "main" method to run the coolTemperature() function at the end of each generation. Again, you may need to adjust the initial mutation rate as it will now function as a max rate depending on the temperature value.

Exercises

1. Use what you know about the simulated annealing heuristic to apply it to crossover rate.

Performance Improvements

Aside from improving the search heuristics, there are other ways to optimize a genetic algorithm. Possibly one of the most effective ways to optimize a genetic algorithm is by simply writing efficient code. When building genetic algorithms that need to run for many thousands of generations, just taking a fraction of a second off of each generation's processing time can greatly reduce the overall running time.

Fitness Function Design

With the fitness function typically being the most processing demanding component of a genetic algorithm, it makes sense to focus code improvements on the fitness function to see the best return in performance.

Before making improvements to the fitness function, it's a good idea to first ensure it adequately represents the problem. A genetic algorithm uses its fitness function to gauge the best area of the search space to focus its search in. This means a poorly designed fitness function can have a huge negative impact on the search ability and overall performance of the genetic algorithm. As an example, imagine a genetic algorithm has been built to design a car panel, but the fitness function which evaluated the car panel did so entirely by measuring the car's top speed. This overly simple fitness function may not provide an adequate fitness value if it was also important that the panel could meet certain durability or ergonomic constraints as well as being aerodynamic enough.

Parallel Processing

Modern computers will often come equipped with several separate processing units or "cores". Unlike standard single-core systems, multi-core systems are able to use additional cores to process multiple computations simultaneously. This means any well-designed application should be able to take advantage of this characteristic allowing its processing requirements to be distributed across the extra processing cores available. For some applications, this could be as simple as processing GUI related computations on one core and all the other computations on another.

Supporting the benefits of multi-core systems is one simple but effective way to achieve performance improvements on modern computers. As we discussed previously, the fitness function is often going to be the bottleneck of a genetic algorithm. This makes it a perfect candidate for multi-core optimization. By using multiple cores, it's possible to calculate the fitness of numerous individuals simultaneously, which makes a huge difference when there are often hundreds of individuals to evaluate per population.

Lucky for us, Java 8 provides some very useful libraries that makes supporting parallel processing in our genetic algorithm much easier. Using *IntStream*, we can achieve parallel processing in our fitness function without worrying about the fine details of parallel processing (such as the number of cores we need to support); it will instead create an optimal number of threads depending on the number of cores available.

You may have wondered why, in Chapter 5, the GeneticAlgorithm calcFitness method clones the Timetable object before using it. When threading applications for parallel processing, one needs to take care to ensure that objects in one thread will not affect objects in another thread. In this case, changes made to the timetable object from one thread may have unexpected results in other threads using the same object at the same time – cloning the Timetable first allows us to give each thread its own object.

We can take advantage of threading in chapter 5's class scheduler by modifying the GeneticAlgorithm's evalPopulation method to use Java's IntStream:

```
/**
    * Evaluate population
    *
    * @param population
    * @param timetable
    */
    public void evalPopulation(Population population, Timetable timetable){
        IntStream.range(0, population.size()).parallel()
        .forEach(i -> this.calcFitness(population.getIndividual(i),
        timetable));

        double populationFitness = 0;

        // Loop over population evaluating individuals and suming
        population fitness
        for (Individual individual : population.getIndividuals()) {
            populationFitness += individual.getFitness();
        }

        population.setPopulationFitness(populationFitness);
    }
```

Now the calcFitness function is able to run across multiple cores if the system supports them.

Because the genetic algorithms covered in this book have used fairly simple fitness functions, parallel processing may not provide much of a performance improvement. A nice way to test how much parallel processing can improve the genetic algorithms performance might be to add a call to Thread.sleep() in the fitness function. This will simulate a fitness function which takes a significant amount of time to complete execution.

Fitness Value Hashing

As discussed previously, the fitness function is usually the most computationally expensive component of a genetic algorithm. Thus, even small improvements to the fitness function can have a considerable effect on performance. *Value hashing* is another method that can reduce the amount of time spent calculating fitness values by storing previously computed fitness values in a hash table. In large distributed systems, you could use a centralized caching service (such as Redis or memcached) to the same end.

During execution, solutions found previously will occasionally be revisited due to the random mutations and recombinations of individuals. This occasional revisiting of solutions becomes more common as the genetic algorithm converges and starts to find solutions in an increasingly smaller area of the search space.

Each time a solution is revisited its fitness value needs to be recalculated, wasting processing power on repetitive, duplicate calculations. Fortunately, this can be easily fixed by storing fitness values in a hash table after they have been calculated. When a previously visited solution is revisited, its fitness value can be pulled straight from the hash table, avoiding the need to recalculate it.

To add the fitness value hashing to your code, first create the fitness hash table in the GeneticAlgorithm class,

```
// Create fitness hashtable
    private Map<Individual, Double> fitnessHash = Collections.
    synchronizedMap(
            new LinkedHashMap<Individual, Double>() {
        @Override
        protected boolean removeEldestEntry(Entry<Individual, Double>
        eldest) {
            // Store a maximum of 1000 fitness values
            return this.size() > 1000;
        }
    });
```

In this example, the hash table will store a maximum of 1000 fitness values before we begin to remove the oldest values. This can be changed as required for the best trade-off in performance. Although a larger hash table can hold more fitness values, it comes at the cost of memory usage.

Now, the get and put methods can be added to retrieve and store the fitness values. This can be done by updating the calcFitness method as follows. Note that we've removed the IntStream code from the last section, so that we can evaluate a single improvement at a time.

```
/**
    * Calculate individual's fitness value
    *
    * @param individual
    * @param timetable
    * @return fitness
    */
    public double calcFitness(Individual individual, Timetable timetable){
        Double storedFitness = this.fitnessHash.get(individual);
        if (storedFitness != null) {
            return storedFitness;
        }
```

```
        // Create new timetable object for thread
        Timetable threadTimetable = new Timetable(timetable);

        threadTimetable.createClasses(individual);

        // Calculate fitness
        int clashes = threadTimetable.calcClashes();
        double fitness = 1 / (double) (clashes + 1);

        individual.setFitness(fitness);

        // Store fitness in hashtable
        this.fitnessHash.put(individual, fitness);

        return fitness;
    }
```

Finally, because we are using the Individual object as a key for the hash table, we need to override the "equals" and "hashCode" methods of the Individual class. This is because we need the hash to be generated based on the individual's chromosome, not the object itself, as it is by default. This is important because two separate individuals with the same chromosomes should be identified as the same by the fitness value hash table.

```
/**
 * Generates hash code based on individual's
 * chromosome
 *
 * @return Hash value
 */
@Override
public int hashCode() {
    int hash = Arrays.hashCode(this.chromosome);
    return hash;
}

/**
 * Equates based on individual's chromosome
 *
 * @return Equality boolean
 */
@Override
public boolean equals(Object obj) {
    if (obj == null) {
        return false;
    }
```

```
    if (getClass() != obj.getClass()) {
        return false;
    }

    Individual individual = (Individual) obj;
    return Arrays.equals(this.chromosome, individual.chromosome);
}
```

Encoding

Another component which can affect the genetic algorithm's performance is the encoding chosen. Although, in theory, any problem can be represented using a binary encoding of 0s and 1s, it's rarely the most efficient encoding to choose.

When a genetic algorithm struggles to converge, it can often be because a bad encoding was chosen for the problem causing it to struggle when searching for new solutions. There is no hard science to picking a good encoding, but using an overly complex encoding will typically produce bad results. For example, if you want an encoding which can encode 10 numbers between 0-10, it would usually be best to use an encoding of 10 integers instead of a binary string. This way it's easier to apply mutation and crossover functions which can be applied to the individual integers instead of bits representing integer values. It also means you don't need to deal with invalid chromosomes such as "1111" representing the value 15 which is beyond our 0-10 required range.

Mutation and Crossover Methods

Picking good mutation and crossover methods is another important factor when considering options to improve a genetic algorithm's performance. The optimal mutation and crossover methods to use will depend mostly on the encoding chosen and the nature of the problem itself. A good mutation or crossover method should be capable of producing valid solutions, but also be able to mutate and crossover individuals in an expected way.

For example: if we were optimizing a function which accepts any value between 0-10, one possible mutation method is *Gaussian mutation* which adds a random value to the gene increasing or decreasing its original value slightly. However, another possible mutation method is *boundary mutation* where a random value between a lower and upper boundary is chosen to replace the gene. Both of these mutation methods are capable of producing valid mutations, however depending on the nature of the problem and other specifics of the implementation, one will likely outperform the other. A bad mutation method might simply round the value down to 0 or up to 10 depending on the original value. In this situation, the amount of mutation that occurs depends on the gene's value which can result in poor performance. An initial value of 1 would be changed to 0 which is a relatively small change. However, a value of 5 would be changed to 10 which is much larger. This bias can cause a preference for values closer to 0 and 10 which will often negatively impact the search process of the genetic algorithm.

Summary

Genetic algorithms can be modified in different ways to achieve significant performance improvements. In this chapter, we looked at a number of different optimization strategies and how to implement them into a genetic algorithm.

Adaptive genetic algorithms is one optimization strategy which can provide performance improvements over a standard genetic algorithm. An adaptive genetic algorithm allows the algorithm to update its parameters dynamically, typically modifying the mutation rate or crossover rate. This dynamic update of parameters often achieves better results than statically defined parameters which don't adjust based on the algorithm's state.

Another optimization strategy we considered in this chapter is multi-heuristics. This strategy involves combining a genetic algorithm with another heuristic such as the simulated annealing algorithm. By combining search characters with another heuristic, it is possible to achieve performance improvements in situations where those characteristics are useful. The simulated annealing algorithm we looked at in this chapter is based on the annealing process found in metallurgy. When implemented in a genetic algorithm, it allows for large changes to occur in the genome initially, then gradually reduces the amount of change allowing the algorithm to focus on promising areas of the search space.

One of the easiest ways to achieve a performance improvement is by optimizing the fitness function. The fitness function is typically the most computationally expensive component, making it ideal for optimization. It's also important that the fitness function is well-defined and provides a good reflection of an individual's actual fitness. If the fitness function gives a poor reflection of an individual's performance, it can slow the search process and direct it towards poor areas of the search space.

One easy way to optimize the fitness function is by supporting parallel processing. By processing multiple fitness functions at a time, it is possible to greatly reduce the amount of time the genetic algorithm spends evaluating individuals.

Another tactic which can be used to reduce the amount of time needed to process the fitness function is fitness value hashing. Fitness value hashing uses a hash table to store fitness values for a number of recently used chromosomes. If those chromosomes appear again in the algorithm, it can recall the fitness value instead of recalculating it. This can prevent tedious reprocessing of individuals that have already been evaluated in the past.

Finally, it can also be effective to consider if improving the genetic encoding or using a different mutation or crossover method could improve the evolution process. For example, using an encoding which poorly represents the encoded individual, or a mutation method which doesn't generate the required diversity in the genome can cause stagnation of the algorithm and lead to poor solutions being produced.

Index

Get the eBook for only $5!

Why limit yourself?

Now you can take the weightless companion with you wherever you go and access your content on your PC, phone, tablet, or reader.

Since you've purchased this print book, we're happy to offer you the eBook in all 3 formats for just $5.

Convenient and fully searchable, the PDF version enables you to easily find and copy code—or perform examples by quickly toggling between instructions and applications. The MOBI format is ideal for your Kindle, while the ePUB can be utilized on a variety of mobile devices.

To learn more, go to www.apress.com/companion or contact support@apress.com.